The Joke is in your Hand!

By: Tim McGrath

WARNING!

The contents of this book is full of inappropriate reading material. It is NOT suitable for children, adults or anyone that is easily offended. This book contains drug and sexual references. It also is full of religious, racist, pedophile, and animal jokes. IT WILL OFFEND ALMOST EVERYONE! If you think that you might be offended by my polluted sense of humor...

Do Not Read!

PREFACE:

I got my sense of humor growing up in New York with a bunch of smart asses. Everyone up there is a comedian. My friends and family are always cracking jokes. We tried to out do each other and find humor in almost everything. From there I served abroad (or two) in the military and ended up in Texas working for the department of redundancy dept.

I think the main differences between my two favorite states is that Texas is hotter and everything is measured in Shitloads. I wasn't sure about the Texans' sense of humor until one told me, "Yankees are like hemorrhoids! When y'all come down and go back up it's no big deal, but when y'all come down and stay down, y'all are a pain in the ass!" (I always thought a Yankee was like a quickie but you're alone.)

Throughout my worldly travels of my youth and now my day to day routine I've traded jokes with almost everyone I know. I didn't make any of this stuff up. None of these jokes are indicative of my feelings on such sensitive issues. These are some of the best and worst jokes I've ever heard. Please use my ammunition from these pages and you can have your audience laughing too. Just don't tell them ALL of these jokes because you'll lose friends like I'm about to.

Thanks to all the joke writers and tellers who let me spread the good humor. I would like to thank all my friends and family for both contributing to this book and putting up with me telling them jokes all of my life. A special thanks to my lovely wife Alison who really didn't appreciate any of them. A word of appreciation to my darling daughters who let me share my computer with them and showed me how to use it. Thanks a million to Billy McGrath for the cover art work. Great job! I would also like to thank Scott Walls for retrieving the lost files on my computer. (Save your work folks!) A big shout out to the person who invented spellcheck. Without whom, none of this would be pussible. Words is hard!

Remember:
If you can't laugh at other people, who can you laugh at?

Jokes are like sex; they're no good if you don't get it.

There's nothing like a good joke! Neither are these...

Other self help books by this author:

Coming soon?

I gained sixty pounds, ask me how.

Learn to talk good.

Turn your family room into a garage in one easy step.

How to turn your friend's crotch into a cup holder.

Design and build your very own Nubian schlong.

Cover design and artwork by Billy McGrath
ID: 3742787
ISBN-13: 978-1468046793

FREE ADVICE!

Never be curious about what the homeless are doing around the corner.
You can't un-see that.

As far as women go...Willing beats pretty!

Don't mistake gay for weakness. You'll get your ass kicked and then your friends will laugh at you.

Just because you're paranoid...
Doesn't mean they're not out to get you.

Don't trust a doctor with a rectal thermometer behind his ear and can't find his pen.

If you want that guy to stop talking to you in the bathroom;
Just say to him, "Nice Dick!"

They say, "Living well is the best revenge."
But stabbing works just fine.

If you see a homeless zero holding a sign that says, "Will work for food."
Give him a coconut.

To catch a Polar bear:
All you have to do is cut a hole in the ice.
Pour a can of peas in a pile next to the hole.
When the Polar bear comes over to take a pee; you kick him in the ice hole.
Or...
You can bend a sharpened bone and pack it in a piece of meat.
Freeze the meat. Throw it on the ice for the Polar bear to eat.
When it swallows the meat, the meat digests and the bone springs open cutting open his guts. Then you can just follow a trail of blood to a dead Polar bear.

Your welcome!

Here are some real, ridiculous, but cool names that I've come across:
If you know any of these people...
Tell them I said, "Ha Ha!"

Hai Ho
Dick Richards
Misty Summer Knight
Uyenchi Ho
Paul Spitznogle
B. M. Easy
S.C. Rhotom
Sue Wu
Jack Schmidt
Rosa Mendosa
Wong Man

Jo King
Ida Dicky
Ikpeaku Iwob
Pat Furbush
Anita Moorehead
Ima Schmuck
John Golightly
Bich Ho
Peter Dong
Sharon Peters
Dick A. Dix

Table of Contents:

JUST FOR KIDS

(Caution! Slow children ahead.)

*   *   *

What do you call a boomerang that doesn't come back?

A stick.

*   *   *

How do you make a tissue dance?

Blow a little boogie in it.

*   *   *

What's Beethoven doing right now?

Decomposing.

*   *   *

What time should you go to the dentist?

Tooth Hurty. (Two thirty.)

*   *   *

A horse walks into a bar and the bartender asks,

"Why the long face?"

* * *

Why was six afraid of seven?

Because seven ate nine.

* * *

What did the termite say when he walked into a bar?

Is the bar tender here?

* * *

What did one snowman say to the other snowman?

Do you smell carrots?

* * *

What do you get when you cross a stream and creek?

Wet feet.

* * *

How do you catch a unique rabbit?

You nique up on it.

* * *

How do you catch a tame rabbit?

Tame way.

*   *   *

How do you know that penguins, cows and zebras are the oldest animals on earth?

They're still in black and white.

*   *   *

A blonde had baby twins. One boy and one girl. She asked her sister to name them.

She named them Denise and Denephew.

*   *   *

What do you call a pig with three eyes?

Piiig.

*   *   *

How many kids with A.D.D. does it take to screw in a light bulb?

Wanna go ride bikes?

*   *   *

A mushroom goes into a bar and the bartender said, "We don't serve your kind in here!"
The mushroom asked, "Why not? I'm a fungi!"

*　　　　*　　　　*

How can you tell a great farmer?

He's outstanding in his field.

*　　　　*　　　　*

Why are gorillas nostrils so big?

They have really fat fingers.

*　　　　*　　　　*

What's invisible and smells like carrots?

Bunny farts.

*　　　　*　　　　*

How do crazy people get through the woods?

They take the psycho path.

*　　　　*　　　　*

What did the fish say when he swam into the wall?

Dam!

ANIMALS

(Taste like food)

* * *

A family of moles wake up one morning and Papa mole runs up to the hole entrance claiming he smells cookies. He calls momma mole over to help locate the smell's origin. Momma mole sticks her head out and claims not to be able to smell cookies. They call the baby mole over to see if he can smell cookies. Both his parents are blocking the hole entrance. He looks up and says, "All I can smell is molasses."

* * *

What do you get if you cross an elephant and a rhino?

El if I know.

* * *

A guy answers his door, looks around, doesn't see anyone and starts to shut the door again when he noticed a snail on his door step. He picked it up and threw it as far as he could across the street. About a year later there's another knock on the door. It was the snail again. It said to the guy, "What the hell was that about?"

* * *

A turtle gets gang raped by a group of snails. The cop asked the turtle if he could identify his attackers. He says, "I don't know, it all happened so fast!"

*   *   *

A baby polar bear asked his mother, "Am I a polar bear?" His mother responds, "Of coarse you're a polar bear." "Are you sure I'm a polar bear?" "Yes! I'm sure you're a polar bear." "Are you positive?" "Yes! I'm positive! Your fur is all white, you live in an ice cave, you eat fish and play on the ice all day. Yes, I'm sure you're a polar bear! Why do you keep asking me that?" He explained, "Because I'm freakin freezing!"

*   *   *

A farmer is getting impatient with the lack of population growth on his pig farm. He goes into town looking for advice. The Veterinarian tells him, ”Take matters into your own hands and take the pigs over the hill, play some romantic music and try to inseminate the pigs himself. You will know they are pregnant when they sleep a lot." The farmer goes home, pours himself a stiff drink and loads the pigs in his truck and takes them over the hill. He comes back a few hours later exhausted. He wakes up the next morning with his muscles aching, looks out the window and sees the pigs running around playing. "Crap!" The farmer has a good breakfast, loads up the pigs in his truck and takes them over the hill again. He returns completely spent. The next day he wakes up, looks out the window and sees that the pigs are going about their normal routine. "Oh no!" He slowly stretches his muscles and loads them up in his truck and tries again. The next day he can barely move. He tells his wife, "I can't sit up to look. What are those pigs doing? Are they still sleeping?" "No," said his wife.

"They're all waiting in your truck and one of them is blowing the horn.”

*   *   *

A rabbit running through the woods finds the deer rolling a joint. “Don’t waste your time with that stuff. Come running with me. You’ll feel better.” They both take off running and come across a giraffe doing some coke. “Come running with us. It’s more fun than that stuff.” They all take off running and see the lion getting ready to shoot up some heroine. The lion smacks the rabbit as soon as he comes near. “Why did you do that?” the others ask. “He was just trying to help us!” The lion says, “Fuck him! Every time he trips on ecstasy, he wants me to go running with him.”

*   *   *

What do you call a cow that had an abortion?

Decaffeinated.

*   *   *

How do you make a cat sound just like a dog?

Douse it with kerosine and set it alight.
WOOF!!

*   *   *

A guy walks into a bar with a monkey on his shoulder. He bellies up to the bar and orders a beer. The monkey gets board, jumps down on the bar starts running up and down eating all the limes and lemons and stuff. The bartender shoes him off. It jumps over onto the pool table to bat around all the balls. The bartender looks up in time to see the monkey swallowing the cue ball. "Hey Buddy! Your monkey just ate one of my pool balls!" "Sorry about that.

He eats everything." He gets up, pays for the beer and throws the barkeep some extra cash for the pool ball, takes his monkey and leaves.

The man comes back a few weeks later with his monkey on his shoulder, bellies up to the bar and orders a beer. The monkey gets board, jumps down on the bar, runs over to the maraschino cherries, pulls one out of the jar, sticks it up his ass, pulls it out and eats it. "Hey!" says the bartender. "Did you see what your monkey just did?" "He just reached into the cherries, pulled one out, stuck it up his ass and then ate it." "Yeah," says the guy. "Ever since he ate that pool-ball last month, now he measures everything first!"

* * *

A pipeline welder gets sent to work in the field out in a middle eastern desert. After a few weeks, he asks the forman what the rest of the guys do for fun. "Well, we just use the local sheep," was his response. The new guy is not impressed with that answer and walks away in disgust.

After another couple of weeks, the new guy is desperate and catches one of the sheep and starts screwing it with wild abandon. When he's done, he turns to find the rest of the workers laughing at him. "I thought all you guys did this," he says embarrassed. They replied, "Yeah, but not with the ugly one!"

* * *

How do you get a dog to stop humping your leg?

Pick him up and suck his dick.

*   *   *

A guy comes home with a duck under his arm and says, "This is the pig I'm screwing."

His wife says, "That's not a pig, it's a duck." The guy says, "I was talking to the duck!"

*   *   *

What do you call a masturbating cow?

Beef stroganoff.

*   *   *

A lizard walking down by the river smells some good weed burning. Looking around for the source he hears the Koala calling his name from up in the tree. "Come on up and try this shit," says the Koala. He and the lizard smoke the whole doobie. The lizard says he needs a drink because his cottonmouth is fierce. He climbs down the tree and onto a rock to position himself on the rivers edge to take a sip. He's so stoned that he losses his balance and falls in. The river swiftly takes him down stream. He manages to pull himself back ashore after a struggle. He's on the bank coughing and spitting up water when an alligator asks him, “What's up?” He tells him about the Koala and his good weed up in the tree and warns him about the cottonmouth. The Alligator walks up to the tree and asks the Koala, who is still smoking, "Got any more of that good stuff?" The Koala looks down at the Alligator and says, “Holy shit! How much water did you drink?"

*   *   *

What do you call a deer with no eyes?

No eye deer. (No idea.)

*   *   *

What do you call a deer with no eyes and no legs?

STILL no eye deer.

*   *   *

What do you call two deer with no eyes and no legs having sex?

Fuckin STILL no eye deer!

*   *   *

A guy goes to get penis enlargement surgery in Africa because no American doctor would mess with his ten inch dick. The doctor in Africa didn't have a prosthetic that would match his girth so he used a baby elephant's trunk. After a short recovery time he traveled back to his girlfriends house to show it off to her. She invited him in to have dinner with her parents. During the meal he started getting an erection while staring at his girlfriend's cleavage. The penis climbed out off his shorts and onto the table. It picked his baked potato off his plate and took it back under the table. The guy sat there with a horrified look on his face hoping nobody else saw it. His dick again reached up and picked his girlfriend's potato off her plate and brought it under the table. Her father asked, "What the hell was that?" The guy had no answer for him. He just sat there looking frightened. Her mom demanded, "Do that again!" He said, "I'd try, but I don't think I can fit another potato up my ass!"

* * *

A beautiful woman stops into a pet shop on the way home from work. She tells the shop owner that she was looking for a pet to keep her company since her husband died. The pet shop owner showed her around the puppies and kittens. The woman said she was looking for something different. "How about a parrot?" "No thanks," she said. "Too noisy." "Well," the proprietor suggested, "We have a pussy eating frog. That should keep you company." "Sounds perfect! I'll take it," she said excitedly. As the shop owner was boxing up the frog he gave her the simple instructions. "Just place him between your legs and tell him what to do."

The woman goes home, lights a candle, dims the lights, disrobes, unwraps the frog and places him between her long legs and says, "Lick." The frog does nothing. "Eat frog, eat!" The frog just croaks. The woman is humiliated. She puts the frog back in the box and takes him back to the pet shop. "This thing doesn't do anything!" The pet shop owner has the lady undress and hop up on the counter. He takes the frog out of the box and says, "Okay Frog, I'm going to show you how to do this just one more time!"

* * *

Jeno and Pete meet up as they're walking their dogs. As they're talking, one dog starts to lick himself. Pete says, "Man, I wish I could do that." Jeno responds, "You could try, but he'd probably bite you."

*   *   *

What's the last thing to go through a flies mind when he hits your windshield?

His asshole.

*   *   *

What do you call a dog with no legs?

It doesn't matter. He won't come anyway.

*   *   *

What do you do with a dog with no legs?

Take him for a drag.

*   *   *

What do Chinese people do with dogs with no legs?

Wok ‘em.

*   *   *

A farmer is growing really concerned about a rooster that he owns. It's having sex with all the other animals on the farm. All of them! Cows, horses, pigs, whatever. It's the horniest thing he's ever seen. He goes into town to talk to the Vet. The doctor tells him not to worry because he'll eventually tire himself out or his heart will quit.

The farmer grabs his feed and other shopping items and returns to the farm. As he pulls into the driveway he sees the rooster motionless in the middle of the the driveway. Well, I guess the doctor was right, he thought. He just screwed himself to death. The farmer gets out of the truck and goes over to the rooster and kicks it a little just to make sure. He goes into the barn to get his shovel. When he returns, he starts to say a prayer for the deceased. The rooster points toward the sky and says, "Shh! Buzzards."

* * *

Why do male elephants have four feet?

So the female elephants can feel something.

* * *

What's long, green and smells like pork?

Kermit's finger.

* * *

A single woman buys herself a parrot to keep her company around the house. When she brings the parrot home, she finds out that the parrot has a very foul mouth. It curses constantly. The woman threatens to put the bird in the freezer if it doesn't behave. "Blow me!" was the birds response. The lady was mortified. She grabbed the bird and put it in the freezer and slammed the door shut. Immediately the bird started yelling, "I'll be good! I'll be good!" She took him out and asked the bird, "Why the change of heart so quickly?" The parrot said, "I saw those chickens in there and realized that you don't fuck around!"

*   *   *

What do you call a bunny with Aids?

Peter Rottentail.

*   *   *

A guy finds an ad on Craigslist for a talking dog. He calls the number in the ad. Since it's just down the street, he goes to have a look. He arrives with skepticism and the owner takes him out back to meet the dog. He asks the dog with a mouth full of sarcasm, "You can really talk?" "Yeah, I can talk," says the dog. "WOW! Holy Crap! You CAN talk!" he shouts in disbelief. "How did you learn how to talk?" The dog begins to tell him that the C.I.A. took him in as a puppy and he was trained at Langley for three years and then he was sent to different parts of the world. “I got close with foreign dignitaries and listened in on their conversations. I'd then report back to my superiors. I've ruined countless terrorist plots against the U.S. and our allies and even prevented wars in eastern Europe.” "Wow, that's remarkable!" "How much do you want for him?" he asks the owner." "I'll sell him to you for fifty bucks." "Fifty dollars? Why so cheap?" His owner says, "Because he's a liar! He's never done any of that crap!"

*   *   *

A guy jogging through the park notices a homeless man on a bench eating dog food. The sight sickens him. The next day he sees the same bum on the same bench, eating dog food out of a can with the same spoon. He stops jogging to tell the man, "That stuff is going to kill you. Dog food isn't made for humans." "Fuck off!" screams the bum. The next day he warns the guy again, "That stuff is going to kill you." "Fuck off!" was the reply again. Day after day for a month, he tries to get the guy to eat something else.

One day the bench is empty. He looks around the park but doesn't see him. He asked another park regular if he'd seen the homeless guy who sits on the same bench and eats dog food out of a can with the same spoon everyday. "Oh, he died." "I told him that dog food was going to kill him!" The other guy says, "It wasn't the dog food. He was sitting on the curb, licking his balls and got hit by a bus."

* * *

Three dogs were in the vets office. The chiwawa was asked by the others, "What are you in for?" "I pissed on my master's brand new carpet, so now I'm being put down." "What are you in for?" they asked the Pitbull. "I chewed up the tires on my master's lawnmower, so now I'm being put down too." "How about you?" the first two asked the German Shepherd. "My master's wife bent over while vacuuming naked. I mounted and humped the hell out of her." "Oh God!" the others said shocked. "So you'll be the first one to die." "Nah." says the Shepherd. "I'm just getting my nails clipped and my teeth brushed."

* * *

A lion is walking through the jungle, hungover and in a bad mood. He comes across the hippo. "Hey Hippo! You ugly piece of shit! Look at you. You're all wrinkly and grey. Your skin's cracking and your ears are too small for your head. Why don't you get lost? Nobody wants to look at you!" The hippo apologizes to the king and moves along disgusted with himself. The lion kind of found that amusing. He came across a giraffe blocking his path. "Hey Giraffe! You overgrown cow! You're hard to look at with your stupid long neck and your weird shaped spots. Take a hike!" "I'm sorry," says the giraffe and he trots off feeling depressed. This is starting to make the lion feel better. He goes over to a frog sitting on a log. "Hey Frog! Why don't you go jump in a lake? Look at you. Your skin's all green and slimy. You got bumps all over you and your yellow eyes look like they're going to pop out of your head." The frog looks up at the lion and says, "Fuck you man! I'm sick!"

* * *

Why would a Panda bear make for a horrible boyfriend?

Because he eats, shoots and leaves

* * *

A guy sitting in the back of a city bus notices, after the last of the other passengers gets off, that the bus driver has a monkey sitting next to him. "Hey! What's with the monkey?" The bus driver checks the mirror to make sure there is no one else on the bus and says, "Check this out!" He leans over and smacks the monkey upside the head. The monkey dives down between the bus drivers legs, pulls down his zipper, pulls out his dick and starts sucking his dick with earnest. The bus driver busts a nut in the monkey's mouth. The monkey wipes off his dick, wipes his own chin, puts his dick away, zips him back up and goes back to his seat. "Wow! That was amazing!" says the passenger. "Whanna see it again?" asks the bus driver. "Sure." The bus driver leans over and cracks the monkey upside the head again. The monkey dives back down between his legs and repeats the whole process. When he's done, he wipes off the bus driver's dick, then his chin and takes his seat again. The guy in the back exclaims, "That was the most awesome thing I've ever seen!" The bus driver asks, "Would you like to try it?" "Sure!" he said. "Just don't hit me so hard!"

*   *   *

Where does virgin wool come from?

Ugly sheep.

*   *   *

Lester bought a mule from his friend James for one hundred dollars. James apologized to Lester when he brought it over because it died. “Just give me my money back.” “Can’t.” said James. “Already spent.” “Leave it here and I’ll just raffle it off.” “You can’t raffle off a dead mule!” cried James. “Sure I can. Watch me.” One week later James asked Lester, “How’d the raffle go?” “Sold four hundred tickets for two dollars a piece.” “Weren’t they mad when they found out it was dead?” “Just the winner,” said Lester. “So I just gave him his two dollars back.”

*   *   *

An ant is walking through the forest when he came across an elephant leaning against a tree in obvious pain. "What's the matter with you Mr. Elephant?" "I got a nasty splinter in my foot and it really hurts." The ant asks, "Would you like me to pull it out for you?" "That would be great!" said the elephant. The ant says, "I'll do it if you let me fuck you in the ass." "Get lost ant! It's not that kind of party." "Suit yourself," says the ant and begins to leave. The elephant thinks about it for a moment and realizes it's just an ant. It won't hurt at all and nobody will see anyway. So he agrees to the deal.

The ant walks over to his foot, reaches up and pulls the sliver of wood with all his might and it slides right out. The elephant is so happy to be able to lower his foot to the ground again. The ant verifies the deal buy saying, "Okay,

I'm going rape your sweet ass now!" The elephant says, "Whatever. Just hurry up." The ant starts walking towards the back of the elephant, gets to his hind leg after a while and begins the long, steep trip up. The elephant is just waiting for him to get done. The ant climbs all the way to his ass and pushes the elephant's tail away. By now the elephant is tired and leans against the tree in boredom. His weight shakes a coconut loose and it falls thirty feet and lands right on top of the elephant's head. He cries, "OW!!!" The ant shouts with pride, "Yeah! Take it all Bitch!"

HUNTING

(Anything for a buck)

* * *

Two Aggie hunters get lost in the woods. After wandering around for hours one remembers something that he read in the hunting manual. If you get lost you should fire shot in the air and wait for help to arrive. He fires a shot and then waits an hour and no help arrives. They fire another shot and wait some more. Nothing. They fire another, then another. They're growing really impatient and it's getting dark now. "Fire another shot," one says to the other. "Okay, but somebody better come soon, I'm running out of arrows."

* * *

Four Polish hunters go to Alaska to do some hunting. Unfamiliar with the area, they drive around looking for some good wilderness access. They see a sign up ahead that reads; 'BEAR LEFT.' So they went home.

*   *   *

Two hunters are just rapping up a long day of not catching anything when one stops to take a leak in the bushes. As soon as he starts to pee, a snake jumps up and bites him right on the head of his dick. He goes down reeling in pain. His friend goes to get help. He runs two miles through the woods to the truck and then drives seven miles into town. He finds the hospital and the doctor tells him he is going to have to go back, suck the poison out of the wound and get him to the emergency room as fast as possible. The guy jumps back into the truck, drives seven miles to the woods, runs two miles back to his buddy's side. His friend, writhing in pain, asked him what the doctor said. “He said, you're going to die!"

*   *   *

One hunter took aim at the bear. His friend kicked off his boots and started putting on his running shoes just in case he missed. “You can’t outrun a bear!” “I don’t have to outrun the bear. I just have to outrun you!”

*   *   *

Hoppy, an Alaskan bush pilot and hunting guide gets hired by some hunters from Texas looking for big game. They bag six moose. Hoppy tells them that the maximum he can take on the plane is four due to weight restrictions. "Bullshit!" say the Texans. "Last year our pilot let us take six and he had the same plane as yours!" Reluctantly, Hoppy lets them load all their catch. The plane can't gain enough altitude to clear the mountains. Only the Texans survive the crash. Climbing out of the wreckage one asked the other, "Where do you reckon we are?" The other Texan says, "Looks like we're near the same spot we crashed last year."

*   *   *

President Obama was out duck hunting with the Bush family on their Texas ranch one day right after the election. Obama shot at and winged his first duck and he and the dogs followed the bird to the fence line. The bird just happened to make it to the other side. Obama put his gun down and climbed over the fence to retrieve his prize.

A good ol' boy pulled up in his rusted out, old, Ford truck. "Whatcha doin' on my land nigga?" Obama couldn't help but laugh at the situation as he began to explain. "I shot a duck and it landed over on your property and I just came over to get it and I'm going to go right back." The redneck, not fond of being laughed at said, "My land. My duck!" "No sir, you don't seem to understand, I shot the duck," said the president. "I don't give a wet fart!" protested the redneck. "My land. My duck! Now get off my property!" Obama, persistent about taking home his first hunting trophy, tried again to explain diplomatically. "Sir, I'm the president of the United States. I shot this duck and I would like to take it back to the White house to have as a trophy."

The redneck who was unimpressed and looking angry, suggested they settle it with something called the 'Three kick game.' Obama requested an explanation. "Well," he began with a spit, "We both get three chances to kick each other. Whoever touches the ground is the loser." Obama thinks for a moment about how good he used to be at soccer back in Kenya. "Okay." With that, the Texan kicked him in the nuts as hard as he could. Obama doubles over in pain but doesn't fall to the ground. He takes a few deep breaths and stands upright again. The Texan uses a side kick right in Obama's knee. That really hurt but the President stands tall. The redneck spins a roundhouse kick and puts the heel of his boot right in Obama's kidney. He screams in pain but doesn't fall to the ground. Obama takes a deep breath and wipes his tears. "Now it's my turn, right?" The redneck says, "Fuck it. Keep the duck!"

MEN
(Poles)

*   *   *

Why does it take a million sperm to fertilize an egg?

None would ask directions.

*   *   *

What's the active ingredient in Viagra?

Fix-A-Flat.

*   *   *

"My husband and I are into S&M now and the sex is been a lot better." "Really?" her long time friend asked. "You're into THAT?" "Yeah. He Snores and I Masturbate."

*   *   *

You think DRUGS are bad for you?

What about that barbitchuate?

*   *   *

How do you turn on a man with a five pound bag of fat?

Put a nipple on it.

*   *   *

Why do men snore when they sleep on on their backs?

Because they get a vapor lock when their balls cover their asshole.

*   *   *

How do you keep your husband from reading your E-mail?

Rename the Mail folder, 'Instruction Manual.'

*   *   *

What's the difference between a G-spot and a golf ball?

A guy will look for a golf ball.

*   *   *

What do you call a really fat guy that's screwing you?

A surround pound system.

*   *   *

Men are like roller coasters.

When they're good you don't want to get off. And when they aren't...
you just want to throw up.

*   *   *

How are men like bank accounts?

Without a lot of money, they don’t generate much interest.

*   *   *

If a man says something in the woods and woman doesn’t hear it.
Is he still wrong?

*   *   *

How many men does it take to screw in a light bulb?

Three. One to screw it in and two to listen to him brag about the screwing part.

*   *   *

Cliff stepped out of the shower. "It's just too hot to wear clothes today," he told his wife, Dee. "What do you think the neighbors would think if I mowed the lawn naked?" She answered, "Probably, that I married you for your money."

*   *   *

Nick decided to help out and do a load of laundry because he wanted a clean sweatshirt for the big game. "Honey, what setting do I put the washing machine on?" His wife Nancy asked, "What does it say on your shirt?"
He replied, "Texas A&M."

WOMEN
(Holes)

*   *   *

My wife is always bitching that I never listen to her.
Or something.

*   *   *

If women ran the world;
We would have a new war every twenty eight days.

*   *   *

How can we trust something that can bleed for a week and NOT DIE?

*   *   *

My wife is a British nymphomaniac.

She has to have it twice a year no matter what.

*   *   *

When I first slept with my wife I could tell that she was inexperienced in bed.

The first thing she did was put her pillow under her ass.

*   *   *

Why is a divorce so expensive?

It's worth it.

*   *   *

How many men does it take to open a beer?

None. She better have it opened when she brings it to you!

*   *   *

What do you do when a woman finally comes out of the kitchen?

Re-secure her chain.

*   *   *

Why do women have little feet?

To stand closer to the sink.

*   *   *

If your dog's barking at the back door and your wife is barking at the front, who do you let in?

The dog. At least he'll shut up once he comes inside.

*   *   *

How are women are like dog shit?

The older they are, the easier to pick up.

*   *   *

What's worse than a male chauvinist pig?

A broad that won't do as she's told!

*   *   *

What do fifty thousand abused women have in common?

They just don’t listen!

*   *   *

What do you say to a woman with two black eyes?

Nothing. She's already been told twice.

*   *   *

What gift do you get for the woman who has everything?

Shelves.

*   *   *

What gift do you get for the woman who has everything including shelves?

Penicillin.

*   *   *

How do you know a woman is wearing pantyhose?

Her ankles swell up when she farts.

*   *   *

What's another way to tell a woman's wearing pantyhose?

Her toes curl up when you screw her.

*   *   *

What's the difference between a woman and a washing machine?

A washing machine doesn't call you constantly after you dump a load in it.

*   *   *

Why do cavemen drag their women by the hair?

When they drag them by the ankles, they fill up with dirt.

*   *   *

Why does it take a menstruating woman an hour to cook minute rice?

IT JUST FUCKIN DOES!!!

*   *   *

Why does pussy smell?

So you can find it in the dark.

*   *   *

Jason tried to pick up a girl in a bar with this line:
"How would you like your eggs in the morning?"

Lisa replied, "Unfertilized."

*   *   *

Why do women fake orgasms?

They think we care.

*   *   *

Why don't women fart?

They can't keep their mouths shut long enough to build up any pressure.

*   *   *

What's the difference between a dick and a hundred dollar bill?

My wife will blow a hundred dollar bill.

*   *   *

What's the difference between a blow job and a sandwich?

If you don't know, lunch is on me.

*   *   *

A biker chick wants to join a real tough, all girl, biker gang. 'The Road Hags.' She goes into their bar, Les'-bos, where they have Jack Daniels on tap. She explains in detail how rough and tough she really is. How she's been riding Harleys since she got kicked out of the fourth grade. How she rolls her own tampons from old carpet. Her L.S.D. diet; take two pills and lose ten days. She even tells about how she gives crabs back to the guys that gave them to her a week earlier, ect. "Okay," the leader says. "We get it. You're tough. We know you can ride, you like drugs and screwing. But have you ever been picked up by the fuzz before?" She said, "Well no. But I've been swung around by the tits a few times."

(Other biker chick gang names: Skanks on Tanks, Menstrual Cycles, Holey Rollers, Hot Twats, Titty Titty Bang Gang, Throttle Hos. Untame Dames, Exhausting Wenches, The Crotch Rockers, Bike Dykes and The Shitfaced Bitches.)

*   *   *

How do you get a woman to stop giving head?

Marry her.

*   *   *

What's the best part about a blow job?

The silence.

*   *   *

How do you rejuvenate a worn out vagina?

Shove in a ham and pull out the bone.

*   *   *

A stranger shows up at this old western town looking for some action. The saloon manager sends him upstairs to talk to the madam. He told the the madam that he was coming off a long ride and would like some rough action from a rugged woman. She hooked him up with Sandpaper Sally. The roughest, toughest, dirtiest girl in the whole wild west. He went to his assigned room and tried to relax when Sandpaper Sally came in with a bottle of beer. She handed him the beer and immediately lifted up her dress, pulled down her knickers and spun around putting her ass high in the air. "Hold on little lady!" he said. "I just got off a long ride. Let me drink my beer first."
"I understand," she said. "That bottle's not a twist off."

*   *   *

Why are tornados named after women?

Because it starts with a blow job and ends up taking your house.

*   *   *

A man walking through the hotel lobby bumps his elbow into the breast of Teri, who was coming out of the elevator. "Pardon me!" the man says. "I know if your heart is as soft as your breast you'll find a way to forgive me."
Teri replied, "If your cock is as hard as your elbow you'll find your way to room 402."

*   *   *

Tom's been trying to get Betty from accounting to go out with him for months but she's always turned him down. Finally after hearing that it's his birthday, she agrees to go to a drive-in movie with him. "No funny stuff!" she insisted. During the flick, he persistently tries to cop a feel, get a kiss, anything. No dice. After the movie is over he tries to get her to go out for a drink to maybe loosen up. She says she needs to go to the bathroom and just wants to go home. Hoping to get this hot chick back to his place; "Well, I don't live too far from here, you could use my bathroom and then maybe we could go do something." "No thanks," she says. "Just pull over next to the woods." She insists, "I just needs to go to the bathroom now and it can't wait." He pulls over knowing that after her pee is over so is this date.

She gets out of the car and says, "No peeking!" and goes into the bushes. He hadn't even considered peeking until she said that, so he decides to at least get a look. He opens his door slowly. He quietly walks around the back of the car to use the headlights to create a silhouette of this beauty. He gets close enough to get a good view. He couldn't believe his eyes! Between her legs was the shadow of a big dick. He'd been duped! All night he's been trying to nail a dude. Pissed off, he runs up and grabs it. "AH HA!" he shouts. She sprang up. "You didn't tell me you were a Peeping Tom!" "Yeah," he says, flicking his hand vigorously. "You didn't tell ME you were taking a Shit!"

* * *

Why do doctors spank babies when they're born?

To knock the dicks off the dumb ones.

* * *

When are fat chicks depressing?

Whenever they're on top.

* * *

James goes into a brothel and asks for the roughest, toughest broad they got. The madam sends him to Sandpaper Sally's room. He undresses upon entry and waits. Sandpaper Sally comes in and climbs on top and mounts him. Immediately he starts complaining that her snatch hurts. She goes into the bathroom and returns a few minutes later and mounts him again. "Ahh," he says. "That feels much better. What did you do?" She says, "I just picked the scabs. Now your riding the puss."

*　　　*　　　*

A woman goes into Walmart with her two kids in tow. The greeter says, "Those are the second set of twins I've seen today." The woman says, "They're not twins. One is four years old and the other is nine. Why would you think they're twins?" The greeter responds, "Because you're too ugly to get laid twice!"

*　　　*　　　*

What do fat chicks and scooters have in common?

They're fun to ride but you don't want your friends to see you on one.

*　　　*　　　*

How many feminist does it take to screw in a light bulb?

Two. One to change it and one to blow me.

*　　　*　　　*

A nude wife blocks the husbands view of the ball game on T.V. "Did you marry me for my body or my mind?"
He answered, "For your sense of humor."

*　　　*　　　*

Smile ladies! It's the second best thing your lips can do!

YOUR MOMMA!
(My Love!)

*   *   *

Your momma's such a nosey tramp.
She contracted snyphilis.

*   *   *

What's the difference between your momma and a rooster?

Your momma says, "Any cock will do!"

*   *   *

Your momma is so fat...
When she walked in front of the T.V.
I missed three commercials.

*   *   *

Your momma is so fat...
When she wears her Malcolm X shirt, helicopters land on her.

*   *   *

Your momma is so fat...
Her genes don't fit.

*   *   *

Your momma is so fat...
When she jogs, she leaves potholes.

*   *   *

Your momma is so fat...
When she wore high heels, she struck oil.

*   *   *

Your momma is so fat...
Her underwear says one size fits four.

*   *   *

Your momma is so fat ...
She can't jump to conclusions.

*   *   *

Your momma's so fat...
She gets taller when she sits down.

*   *   *

Your momma's so fat...
Her nickname is DAMN!

*   *   *

Your momma's so big...
I have to climb her every month with a gallon of paint to defend my sister's honor.

*   *   *

Your momma's nose is so flat...
She can eat a wall.

*   *   *

Your momma's toenails are so long...
Her neck is always bleeding.

*   *   *

Your momma's menstrual cycle is marinara sauce.

*   *   *

Your momma is like a vacuum cleaner...
She sucks, she blows and she carries her own bags.
Then she gets laid in the closet.

*   *   *

Your momma's breath stinks so bad...
When she smokes she blows onion rings.

*   *   *

Your momma's like a record album...
She's an old, dusty, flat, black with a hole in it.

*   *   *

Your momma's so black...
When she got in my car, my friends thought I got tinted windows.

*   *   *

Your momma's so black...
When I kicked her out of my car, my oil light came on.

*   *   *

I saw your momma selling potato chips...
She was standing on the corner yelling, "Free-lays, Free-lays!"

*   *   *

Your momma's hung like a tire tube.

*   *   *

Your momma's so stoopid...
She couldn't turn on the computer because she can't find the ANY key.

*   *   *

Your momma's so fat...
When I climbed on top of her, I got a nose bleed.

*   *   *

I rolled over twice and was still on top.

*   *   *

Your momma snacks on Wheat Thicks.

*   *   *

Your momma's so ugly...
She looks like she's been bobbing for french fries.

*   *   *

Your momma's so ugly...
The tide won't take her out.

*   *   *

Your momma's snatch is so hairy...
You were born with a carpet burn.

*   *   *

Your momma's crabs have lice.

*   *   *

Your momma uses a rolled up mattress for a tampon.

*   *   *

Your momma calls her tampons Manhole covers.

*   *   *

Your momma's bra's are now lactose intolerant.

*   *   *

Your momma looks like I need a drink.

*   *   *

Your momma's so bowlegged...
I hang her over my door for good luck.

*   *   *

Your momma's so bowlegged...
She can walk in corduroys without making noise.

*   *   *

Your momma's been picked up so much...
She has handles.

*   *   *

Your momma's such a whore...
She's going to be buried in a Y shaped coffin.

*   *   *

Doing your momma is like fucking the world.
Ever stick your dick out an open window?

*   *   *

Your momma is perfect...
Pistol grip ears, a flat head so I can rest my drink,
her teeth retract and her tonsils shoot Vaseline.

*   *   *

Your momma is like a mosquito...
You have to smack her to get her to stop sucking.

*   *   *

Your momma's vibrator has a kick start.

*   *   *

Your momma doesn't like using her vibrator though.

It chips her teeth.

*   *   *

Your momma's teeth have so many gaps...
It looks like her tongue is in jail.

*   *   *

Your momma's so ugly...
She scared the shit out of the toilet.

*   *   *

Your momma went to Hollywood to become an actress.
She blew her big chance and still didn't get the part.

*   *   *

Your momma's like a bowling ball...
She gets picked up, fingered and thrown in the gutter.

*   *   *

I was going down on your mother and she came carrots and peas. I jumped back in horror and yelled, "What are you sick or something?"
She said, "No, the guy before you was!"

*   *   *

Okay, I'll lay off your momma.
Lord knows she's been laid on enough.

HAPPY COUPLES
(Stale Mates.)

* * *

The secret to a happy marriage...
Nobody wears the pants.

* * *

A woman comes home after a long, hard day at work and tells her husband, "Take off my dress!" He takes off her dress for her. "Now, take off my high heels!" He complies. "Now, take off my bra!" He clumsily does as he's told. "Now remove my lace panties!" He follows her orders. Then she says, "Don't let me catch you wearing my clothes again!"

* * *

A woman is sick of her husband's flatulence during the night. His farts are so fierce she tells him that one day he's going to blow his guts out. He thinks it's funny. She does not. One morning after a sickening display of a gas attack during the night, she decides to have some fun with him. She goes into the kitchen trash and gets some of the chicken guts from last night's dinner and carefully slips them into his pajama bottoms. She soon hears his blood curdling scream coming from the bedroom. She can barely control her laughter when her husband appears with a horrified look on his face. "What's the matter honey?" she asks innocently. "You were right, I farted my guts out." "Oh my, what should we do?" she said shaking from her containment of laughter. "Don't worry," he said calmly. "By the grace of God and theses two fingers, I was able to get them back in."

*   *   *

A wife asks her husband during a quite diner. "If I died, would you remarry?" "I suppose I would. There's no sense spending the rest of my life alone." After a pause, she agrees. "But would you two stay in OUR house?" "Sure. It's almost paid for." "I guess your right," she says meekly. "Would you let her have my car?" "I don't see why not. It's runs great and has low miles." "What about my golf clubs? Would you let her use those too?" "Nah," he says. "She's a lefty."

*   *   *

An elderly couple were driving when they got pulled over by a cop. "Why are you folks speeding?" asked the cop. "What did he say?" asked the old lady from the passenger side. "He wants to know why we're going so fast!" He turned to the cop and told him that his wife is annoying the shit out of him and he just wants to get there as soon as possible. "Where are you coming from?" asked the cop. "What did he say?" The man says to his wife, "He wants to to know where we live!" He says to the cop, "Victoria." The cop asked, "Where are you two headed?" "What did he say?" asked the lady. "He asked where we are headed!" shouts the old man. He turns to the cop and tells him, "Elmer. It's my wife's hometown." The cop said, "I knew a girl from Elmer. The worst fuck I ever had." "What did he say?" asked the lady. The husband says, "He thinks he knows you!"

*   *   *

A guy calls his girlfriend from the hospital. "Honey, I cut off my finger at the factory."
She asked, "The whole finger?"
He said, "No! The one next to it."

*   *   *

A wealthy businessman called home and his Hispanic maid answered. "Where's my wife?" he asked. The maid answered hesitantly, "I thought she was in bed with you." The guy blows his lid. "I knew that bitch was cheating on me! Look, I will double your salary if you do me a favor. Go into my desk draw, get my gun and shoot them both in the head." "I don't think I can do that senior." "Okay," he says. "I will triple your salary and you can have my wife's car." "Si senior, I will do it." The guy can hear the gunfire over the phone. BLAM! BLAM! She came back to the phone, "Senior, I did it. They are dead." "Good," he says. "Now roll them up in the rug and drag them out by the pool. I will deal with them when I get home." There was silence on the line. "Finally, she cleared her throat and said softly, "But senior, you don't have a pool."
He responded, "Is this 631-555-1349?"

*   *   *

A newlywed husband tells his bride, “If you want to have sex, just pull on my penis. If you don’t, just pull on it eighty times.”

*   *   *

A woman wakes up and her husband is pouring crushed aspirin in her mouth. "What the hell are you doing?" "I'm taking care of your headache," he exclaimed. "But I don't have a headache!" He said, "Good! Lets screw!"

*   *   *

What's 'making love?
It's something my wife does while I'm fucking her.

*   *   *

A husband and wife were on separate phone lines for a radio contest. All that was required of them was to answer the same five questions the same way and they win a week long cruise. With his wife's line muted, the husband went first. His first question was: “What did your wife wear on your first date?” He answered: “A red dress.”
The second was: “Where did you go on your first anniversary?”
He answered: “Red Lobster.”
The third question: “What was the color of your first can of paint you bought as a couple?”
He was relieved that he remembered the answer: "Red," he said begrudgingly.
His forth question: “WHEN was the last time you two had sex?”
That, he was proud to answer. "Today! It was this morning, before I left for work."
His last question: “WHERE was the last place you two had sex?” With a chuckle, "On the kitchen table after breakfast," he said smugly.
Now it was the wife's turn. She answered the the first three questions without hesitation. The forth question kind of threw her. She was sheepish to say, "This morning?" The fifth and last question of... “WHERE did you last have sex?” produced silence on her end of the phone. "Honey, just answer the question." "No!" she sad adamantly. "This is for a nice trip," said the DJ. "No way! My parents might be listening." "So what? This is for that cruise that we always wanted to go on," begged her husband. The DJ's are laughing. They said that they'll even throw in five hundred dollars spending money if she answers. "Come on Honey. Just tell them where. Please!" begged her husband. "All right!" she said. After a long pause she finally answered..."In the ass."

*   *   *

A guy who almost forgot his daughters birthday runs into the toy store frantic for a great gift. The sales girl asks if he would like some help. "I need a present for a nine year old girl." "Okay. How about a Barbie? All little girls like Barbie. Come on I'll show you." She takes him to where they have a whole isle with nothing but Barbie dolls and Barbie accessories. The guy is overwhelmed. The girl walks him through it.

"This is your basic Barbie doll. $19.99. This is Party Barbie. It comes with sunglasses and a beach ball. $29.99. This is Ballroom Barbie. It comes with three beautiful dresses. $59.99. Over here we have Wedding Barbie. It comes with a white wedding gown, and a horse drawn carriage. It's on sale for $79.99. The best one is Divorced Barbie though, it's only $299.99." "299.99!?" The guy repeats in disbelief. "Why so much?" "Well," she says, "It comes with Ken's car, Ken's boat, Ken's dream house...."

*   *   *

Why do husbands die before their wives?

They want to.

*   *   *

A man and wife go to a marriage counselor to discuss their problems. The counselor asks the man to name one thing that they still have in common.
He says, "Neither one of us sucks dick!"

*   *   *

A husband and wife were going over all the bills that were spread out on the kitchen table. The husband says, "We're a sinking ship! We're going to have to go to plan B." "What's plan B?" asked the wife. "Well, I'm working two jobs and you're working full time; I think you need to earn us some extra cash on your back." "What? Prostitution? I can't do that!" screams his wife. "I don't like it any more than you do but we're going to lose the house and cars." After a long talk and a lot of crying, she agreed since he promised to be near her the whole time.

He gets her dressed up like a skank and stands her out on the corner. He hides in some nearby bushes. "A car is coming," she says nervously towards the bushes. "Go see what they want," says her husband. She clumsily walks with her four inch high heels and leather mini skirt over to the car and asked the guy what he wants. "How much?" "Hold on," she says. Clip, clip, clip, clip, with her high heels, over to the bushes. She whispers, "He wants to know how much." "Tell him fifty bucks," says her husband. Clip, clip, clip, clip, back to the car. "Fifty bucks." "I only have thirty five bucks," says the John. "Hold on." She goes back over to the bushes. "He says he only has thirty five dollars." Her husband says, "Tell him that you'll give him a blow job for thirty five." Clip, clip, clip, clip, back to the car. "I'll give you a blow job for thirty five." "Okay. Get in." She gets in the passenger side and they start fooling around. She reaches in his pants and pulls out the biggest dick she's ever seen in her life. A one eyed monster! "Hold on," she says. She gets out of the car and goes over to the bushes and whispers, "Hey! Do you have fifteen bucks I can borrow?"

*   *   *

Jamie and Chris were talking over a beer. Jamie says, "I made a Freudian slip the other day." "What's that?" asked Chris. "Well, it's like when you mean to say one thing, but say something dirty instead. Like Monday, I was at the train station and I asked the window clerk for a picket to Titsburgh." "Oh, I get it," said Chris. I made a Freudian slip too. At breakfast this morning, I meant to ask my wife if she could please pass the butter but instead I said,
"You fucking bitch! You ruined my life!"

*   *   *

A man answers his door when his neighbor is furiously banging on it. "What's the hubbub Juan?" Juan shouts, "Your freakin' son has been peeing his name in the snow all over my yard." "So what? All little boys pee their name in snow. Why are you so mad about that?" His neighbor yelled, "It's in my daughter's handwriting!"

*   *   *

A guy is shopping in the grocery store and notices a pretty woman looking at him. He ignores her and turns into the next isle. He sees her again and she waves. "I'm sorry. Do I know you?" he asks. She says, "I think you're the father of one of my kids." He pours through his mental rolodex trying to think who this woman could be. Finally it hits him. "Oh my God! Your that hooker that I nailed against the dumpster behind Chucky-Cheese two years ago during my sons birthday party?" "No!" she responded. "I'm his math teacher!"

*   *   *

The doctor tells a woman that her husband illness has progressed rapidly and he's not going to make it through the night. She goes to his bedside and asked if there was anything she could do to make him more comfortable. "Well, I'd like to have sex." She climbs on top of him and gives him what he needs. Later, it's a little after midnight and he can't sleep. He asked her if they can do it again. She climbs on top of him and they do it for twenty minutes more. At about two thirty she asked him if there is anything he would like. He says, "I feel great. Can we do it one more time?" She says, "You know; some of us have to get up in the morning!"

*   *   *

A king goes away and leaves his beautiful daughter in the protection of his trusty guards. However, he doesn't trust them THAT much. He has his daughter fitted with a chastity belt that has razor blades. After the king returns, he assembles the guards to check their penises. The first one's dick was a mangled mess. The king had him executed. He checked the next guard and his prick was just a bloody nub. He too, was executed. He called upon his last guard for inspection. His penis was perfectly intact. The king was elated. "I hereby dub you a knight. You will be the protector of my family, and if you like, you may have my daughters hand in marriage. What do think about that?" The guard responded, "Emphf. Mmumpf!"

*   *   *

You heard the story of Lorrena Bobitt cutting off her husbands penis and throwing it out of her car window. Well, the part you didn't hear was where it landed. It actually stuck to the windshield of the car behind her. The horrified father who was driving with his young daughter in the front seat quickly turned on the windshield wipers to get it off. "What was that?" asked the wide eyed little girl. "That was a bug," the dad replied quickly. She asked, "Did you see the size of the dick on that thing?"

*　　　　*　　　　*

Louetta, Lorrena Bobitt's sister, tried the same thing with her asshole husband. Except she missed and accidentally stabbed him in the leg. The police charged her with a Misdewiener.

*　　　　*　　　　*

An accountant gets a tattoo of a hundred dollar bill on his penis. His wife asked him why he would do such a thing. "Three reasons," he replied. "One: I like to watch my money grow. Two: I like to play with my money.
Three: Next time you want to blow a hundred dollars you won't have to go to the mall!"

*　　　　*　　　　*

A lady responds to the front door bell in her robe just as she was getting out of the shower. It's the neighbor Mike, looking for her husband Bob. She tells him that he's not home at the time. Before Mike leaves he has a thought. "Hey Diane, I was just thinking. Please don't be offended by this but I've always admired your breasts. I know you guys are hurting financially right now with you being out of work and all. I was just wondering if I could see them. I'll give you a hundred dollars." At first, she was appalled. But she knows he's right and ashamedly complies. He stares wide eyed at the most perfect pair he's ever seen. "Diane," he stammers, "I'll give you another hundred if you let me kiss them." Knowing that money is a real issue right now, she agrees. She takes the other hundred and holds open her robe for Mike to suckle on her. Mike comes up for air and says, "Diane, I've got to have you! I'll give you another hundred if you let me make love to you." "No!" she says. "That's enough!" "I'll give you two hundred dollars more if you let me have you right now." "No!" she says insistently. "Look." Mike says digging in his wallet "Three hundred dollars. I promise I'll be fast." Wow! That's five hundred dollars. We sure could use that money she thinks to herself. "Okay. Just be quick about it," she says. Mike takes her furiously on the living room floor. He gets done and limps home. Bob comes home a few minutes later and asks Diane if she'd seen Mike at all. "Why?" Diane asks nervously. "Well, he was supposed to come over today to return the five hundred dollars he borrowed."

* * *

A guy comes home and finds his wife packing a suitcase. "Where are you going?" "I'm going to Las Vegas! I just saw on the T.V. that the hookers out there are getting paid five hundred dollars a trick. Why should I stay around here and do it for free?" The husband grabs a bag and starts putting his clothes in it. The wife asked, "Where are you going?" "I'm going to Vegas with you. I want to see you try to survive on two thousand dollars a year."

* * *

After twenty years of having sex in the dark the wife finds out her husband has been using a strap-on with her the whole time. Angry, she storms into the living room with the evidence. "Explain the dildo you bastard!" He calmly replied, "Explain the kids."

*   *   *

A newlywed couple goes to a fancy hotel. Upon check-in the woman in reception asked, "Are there any reservations?" He said, "Yeah. She won't do anal!"

*   *   *

A man and his wife are watching the Science channel. It was an episode about mixed emotions and being in two minds about things. The guy says to his wife, "This is a load of crap! There's nothing you can tell me that can make me happy and sad at the same time." His wife says, "Oh yeah? Your dick is bigger than all your friends!"

*   *   *

A married couple were watching a documentary on television about a West African tribe that attaches weights to their penises to make them longer. They can stretch them up to twenty four inches. The wife tells her husband that he should try it. The next day he ties a weight to his penis. A couple of days later the wife asked her husband if it's working. He says, "I'm halfway there." "Really? It's twelve inches already?" "No," he says. "It's turning black."

*   *   *

While watching a porno, the husband acknowledges the overzealous actress and asks his wife, “How come I never hear YOU scream like that when YOU have an orgasm?” She replied, “Because YOU’RE never home.”

* * *

Myles was flipping the channels back and forth between the fishing network and the porn channel. His wife, becoming more and more annoyed said, “For Goodness’ sake! Leave it on the porn channel. You already know how to fish.”

* * *

Greg was drinking in the bar and the bartender noticed that after every drink, he would look in his shirt pocket and then order another drink. This went on all night. Finally the bartender asked him, “What’s in your shirt pocket?” Greg said, “It’s a picture of my wife. I’m going to keep drinking till she looks good, then I’ll go home.”

* * *

The father of the groom said to his son, “Congratulations my boy. Your going to remember today as the happiest day of your life.” “But I’m not getting married until tomorrow.” His dad says, “I know. That’s what I mean!”

* * *

A guy is fishing on a pier when one of the locals asked him if he was new to the area. "No, I'm here on my honeymoon." "Honeymoon?" the local gasped.
"I don't mean to be rude buddy, but shouldn't you be back in the hotel room nailing your bride?" "Nah, she's got Gonorrhea." "So? Flip her over and tap that ass."
"Can't," said the groom. "She's got diarrhea." "Then make her give you some head or something!" "Nah, she's got gingivitis too." "Damn son! Why did you marry this girl?"
"Well, she's got worms too; and I love to fish!"

LITTLE JOHNNY
(lil' shit)

*　　　　*　　　　*

The kids in little Johnny's class are reviewing all the animals and the noises they make. The teacher goes up and down the rows asking each student what sound the animal makes when she she calls them out. "Mary, what sound does a duck make?" "Quack," says Mary. "Good," says the teacher. "Bobby, what sound does the cow make?" "Moo," says Bobby. "Good. Okay Johnny, what sound does a pig make?" Johnny replied, "On the ground Mother-Fucker!!!"

*　　　　*　　　　*

A woman notices Little Johnny washing down his second candy bar with a second can of Coke. "You know, too much sugar is really bad for you." Johnny told her, "My Grandpa lived to be one hundred and two years old." "Did your Grandpa eat two candy bars and drink two Cokes everyday?" Johnny said, "No! He minded his own damn business!"

*　　　　*　　　　*

Little Johnny asked his mom, "Where do babies come from?" His mom replied, "The stork brings them." Johnny said, "I know! But who fucks the stork?"

*   *   *

Little Johnny and his brother Jimmy come down stairs for breakfast. Mom asks, "What would you like?" Jimmy says, "How about some fucking french toast?"
Mom flips out! She grabs him by the throat, shoves his head into the wall and smacks his face repeatedly with both hands. Dad pulls him over his knee and beats him with his belt for about five minutes. Jimmy goes running upstairs crying hysterically. Johnny's mom asks him what he would like for breakfast. Johnny says, "You can bet your ass I don't want the fucking french toast."

*   *   *

A priest walks by and sees little Johnny sitting on the curb with a glass jar. "What do you have there?" "Well father, this is the most powerful liquid on earth." "Holy water?" "No. Turpentine," said Johnny. "I'm sorry, but you're mistaken. Holy water is the most powerful liquid on earth," the priest said. "If you rub a dab of holy water on a woman's belly she'll pass a baby boy." Johnny said, "Maybe, but if you rub a dab of turpentine on a cat's ass, it'll pass a motorcycle."

*   *   *

Little Johnny came home from school and his mom asked him how it went. Little Johnny was very excited to tell his mom, "I finally answered one of the teachers questions today." "Really? What was the question?" Johnny replied, "Who farted?"

*   *   *

It's first day of first grade and Little Johnny has been using foul language all day. The class has just reviewed the alphabet and the teacher wants them to do an exercise. The students say the letter and a word that begins with that letter. "Who wants to go first?" the teacher asked. All the kids, including Johnny, raise their hand. "Mary," the teacher calls. "A. Apple." "Very good Mary. Who wants to go next?" All the kids raise their hands. "Bobby." "B. Boy." "Very good Bobby." Johnny wants to go next but the teacher is afraid that he's going to use a curse word so she's avoiding him with the obvious letters. It's now unavoidably. It's Johnny's turn. It's the letter R. The teacher wonders what's the worst thing he can say? She calls on him. "Johnny." "R. Rat." "Very good Johnny." Johnny continues, "A big fucking rat, with a cock about a foot long!"

*   *   *

Little Johnny's neighbors just had a baby and it was born without any ears. Johnny's family is going to visit. Little Johnny's father warns him not to say anything about the baby not having any ears or he'll get a beating. They bring the neighbors a gift and admire the newborn. Little Johnny peeks over the top of the crib and says, "Wow! She has big eyes. Can she see okay?" Yes, was the reply from the proud parents. "Good." Johnny says. "Because if she needs glasses, she's fucked!"

*   *   *

Little Johnny was called on by his teacher to answer, "Who signed the Declaration of Independence?" "I don't know and I don't give a fuck," was Johnny's response. The teacher had enough of his constant cursing. She marched

Johnny straight to the principal. In front of the principal she again asked Johnny, "Who signed the Declaration of Independence?" "I don't know and I don't give a fuck," Johnny said again. They called Johnny's father to the school. In front of him, they asked Johnny again, "Who signed the Declaration of Independence?" "I don't know and I don't give a fuck," was Johnny's response again. Johnny's father smacked the shit out of him. "Boy, if you signed that fucking paper you better own up to it!"

* * *

When Little Johnny got home from school his mother asked him what he did today. Johnny told her, "I had sex with my teacher." "What? Go to your room!"

When dad got home from work his wife tells him to ask Johnny what he did in school today. Dad says, "So, Johnny, what did you do in school today?" "Well, I had sex with my teacher." "What? That's great! I didn't get laid until I was nineteen. I'm so proud of you! I'm going to buy you that bike you've been wanting and we'll go for a ride." Johnny said, "Not today dad. My ass is killing me!"

* * *

Little Johnny walked in on his parents humping away in their bedroom and immediately turns and leaves. They are both really embarrassed. The father goes to talk to him about what he just saw and explain the birds and the bees. Dad goes to Johnny's room but he's not there. He checks the den, the kitchen and the bathroom but he can't find him anywhere. He hears some noises coming from Grandma's room, opens the door and sees Johnny on top of Grandma repeating what he just saw his parents doing. His father shouts in disgust, "Johnny! Stop!" Johnny says, "Yeah, it's not so nice when it's YOUR mom is it?"

*   *   *

The neighbor sees Little Johnny digging a hole and asked what he's doing. "My goldfish died." "Why are you digging such a big hole for a goldfish?" Johnny answered, "Because it's in your fucking cat!"

*   *   *

Dad told little Johnny to run out to the car and get his smokes. The boy returns with a box of condoms instead. The shocked father tells him to put those back and try again. The boy inquires what condoms are. The quick thinking dad explains that they are rain covers to keep his cigarettes dry. The next day is dad's birthday, so little Johnny runs down to the drugstore with his piggy bank and asks the pharmacist for some condoms. Amused that a first grader wants rubbers, she jokingly asks what size he needs. Little Johnny responded, "Big enough to fit a Camel."

*   *   *

The teacher asked Little Johnny if he knows a multi-syllable word. He answered, "Mas-tur-bate." "Wow Johnny. That's a mouthful." Johnny says, "No, you're thinking of a blowjob."

*   *   *

Miss Linda, asked the kids of her first grade class to bring in ten dollars for the class pictures tomorrow. All the kids groaned. Miss Linda told them that they will appreciate these pictures when they grow up. "You can look at these some day and say, There's Terry, she's a lawyer now, or there's Billy, he's a doctor." Johnny shouted from the back, "There's Miss Linda, she's dead now!"

*   *   *

Little Johnny's class was reviewing famous quotes. The teacher told them that since it's a three day weekend they can leave early if they answer the question correctly. "Who said, "The only thing we have to fear is fear itself?" Mary raised her hand. "Yes Mary?" "Franklin D. Roosevelt." "Very good Mary, you're excused." "Who said, "Ask not what your country can do for you, ask what you can do for your country?" "John F. Kennedy." Bobby said. "Excellent, you too may leave for the weekend." Little Johnny is dying to answer one so he can get out of there. He's waving his hand like crazy. The teacher is calling on everyone but him and one by one they are leaving. Out of frustration, Johnny shouted out, "Where the fuck did all those Mexicans come from?" "Who said that?" yelled the teacher. Johnny said, "Davy Crockett at the Alamo! See you Tuesday!"

*   *   *

Little Johnny called to his younger brother, "Come up stairs quick! Be quiet." He points to their parents bedroom door. "Look through the keyhole." The little boy bends down. He gasps in horror as he looks in. Johnny says to him, "Can you believe that's the same woman who just last night, beat you for sucking your THUMB?"

*   *   *

Little Johnny is doing poorly in school. His parents called in tutors as well as stay after school lessons, but it didn't help. Johnny's parents enrolled him into a Catholic school. Johnny's grades immediately improved. His parents asked him what was the cause of his remarkable turn around. Johnny replied, "As soon as I saw that guy nailed to the plus sign, I figured they weren't fucking around!"

*　　　　*　　　　*

Little Johnny's mom was cleaning Johnny's room and found a bondage, S&M magazine in his closet. She promptly showed it to his father. She asked, "What do you think we should do about this?" Johnny's father looked through the mag and said, "Well, I don't think we should spank him."

*　　　　*　　　　*

Little Johnny goes to the zoo with his parents. He points to the elephant and asked his mother, "What's that thing hanging down?" His mother responded, "Oh that's his trunk." Johnny says, "No, not that! What's the thing hanging down between his legs?" His mother shamefully brushes the question off, "Oh, that's nothing." Johnny asked his father, "What's that thing hanging between the elephant's legs?" His father said, "That's his dick." Johnny told him, "Mom said it was nothing." Johnny's father replied, "Your mom's spoiled."

*　　　　*　　　　*

Little Johnny has a new substitute teacher for the rest of the week. She's young and very pretty. She asked Johnny why he was smiling. "Because I'm in love." "With whom?" "With you," Johnny answered. Flattered, the teacher explained to Johnny, "Don't you see how silly that is? Some day I hope to have a husband of my own but I don't want a child." Little Johnny said, "Don't worry. I'll wear a rubber!"

*　　　*　　　*

While learning about the founding fathers, the teacher asked Little Johnny if he knew why George Washington's father didn't punish him for chopping down his cherry tree. Johnny said, "Because he was holding a fucking axe!"

*　　　*　　　*

Little Johnny has the day off from school and is driving his mom nuts while she's trying to clean house. "Go out and play!" "There's no one around," he says. "Well, they're building a house across the street, go talk to the carpenters, maybe you'll learn something," his mom suggested.

Johnny doesn't come home until six thirty. "Where have you been?" "You said to go talk to the carpenters. You said I might learn something." "What did you learn then?" "I learned how to hang a door," Johnny said proudly. "That's great! How do you hang a door?" "Well, you hang the door up and if it doesn't fit, you take the son of a bitch down, plane some shit off and you hang the mother-fucker back up." Mom gets so angry she sends Johnny to his room until dad comes home. "Ask your son what he did today!" Dad goes up to Johnny's room and asked him what he did. "I learned how to hang a door from the carpenters across the street." "That's great son! How do you hang a door?" "Well, you hang the door up and if it doesn't fit, you take the son of a bitch down, plane some shit off and hang the mother-fucker back up." Dad shouts,

"That language will not be tolerated in this house! You must be punished! Go outside and get me a switch!" Johnny said, "Fuck you! That's an electricians job!"

BAR ROOM

(Mommy, that man smells like tinkle.)

*　　　*　　　*

A guy goes into a bar that he's never been in before to watch the game on TV. The game gets kind of boring after a while and the guy keeps getting distracted by a big jar of money behind the bar. He asks the bartender what's up with the jar and the bartender tells him it's a contest prize. He'll have to put twenty dollars in the jar to find out the rules. "No thanks," he says, and goes back to watching the game. Before long, the game on the tube is a lopsided affair and is really dull. The guy is kind of buzzed now and really curious about that contest. "Okay!" He asks the bartender, while handing over his twenty, "What's the deal with the money?" "Well," the bartender begins, "Who ever successfully completes three tasks can have all the money in the jar. First, you have to chug this whole bottle of tequila in one shot. No puking. Two; you have to go out back and remove an abscess tooth from my pit bull's mouth. Then, screw the ugly, old lady that lives upstairs and all this money is yours." The guy who has never been much of a tequila drinker lost interest as soon as he heard step one.

After a while, the game on T.V. is over and the guy is pretty drunk. He goes to pay his tab and takes one more look at the big jar that now contains his money. That's a lot of money he thinks to himself. "You know what?" he says to the bartender, "I'm gonna give it a shot!" The bartender rings a bell and calls the whole bar's attention to the new guy whose going to go for the money. The place erupts with applause and everyone gathers around. The guy takes a few deep breaths and turns the tequila bottle upside down, chugging the whole thing. Everyone cheers in disbelief. The guy stumbles towards the back door falling down twice. It takes him a couple of tries to turn the door knob. He finally makes it out, shutting the door behind him. Immediately there's a lot of growling, barking, yelling and screaming. A couple of big crashes and then some loud yelping. The door swings back open and the guy falls through the doorway covered in blood and sweat and his clothes are torn to shreds. He picks himself back up and says, "Now, where's that old bitch with the bad tooth?"

* * *

Mary goes into a dive bar and orders a Budweiser. She drinks half of it and passes out. The bartender and his friend are the only other people in the place so they take her into the back room, put her on the pool table and take turns screwing the hell out of her. The next day she comes back in and orders a Budweiser. She drinks about half the bottle and passes out again. The bartender and his friend, plus a couple of other guys, carry her into the back room, put her on the pool table and screw the hell out of her. Mary comes in again the next night and there is about two dozen guys in there. She sits down orders a Bud, drinks half, passes out, and gets screwed buy every guy in the place. When she returns the fourth night, the place is wall to wall men waiting for their turn with her. She sits down and the bartender asks, "The usual?" Mary says, "No, make it a Miller. Budweiser makes my pussy sore."

* * *

Two guys are drinking in a bar when one orders shots. His friend tries to stop him. "If my wife finds out that I got drunk she'll kill me." "Relax," says his buddy. "Just a couple of shots. We've only had a few beers so far, a couple of shots ain't going to bust you." The guy agrees and after a toast, gulps the shot down. Unfortunately, it goes down wrong and he upchucks a little and gets some on his shirt. "Crap!

Now my wife is going to find out for sure!" "Calm down," says his friend. "She doesn't have to know you got drunk. Just put a twenty in your shirt pocket and tell her some drunk puked on your shirt and gave you the twenty for the dry cleaning." "Hey! That's pretty smart," he says. They carry on drinking. They end up getting hammered and make their way home. The married guy wakes up the next morning with his wife screaming at him. "You sorry son of a bitch! You got drunk at the bar last night didn't you?" "No!" says the guy defiantly. "Bullshit!" says his wife. "You puked on your shirt." "No! That wasn't me. Somebody else threw up on me. Look in my shirt pocket, there's twenty dollars in there. They gave me that for the dry cleaning." She looks in his shirt pocket and says, "There's forty dollars in here." "Yeah," he says. They shit my pants too!"

* * *

A man orders six shots and dumps them down fast. "You would drink like this too if you had what I had." "What do you have?" asked the bartender. "Fifty cents."

* * *

A guy is going through a nasty divorce and his wife's lawyer is taking him to the cleaners. On top of that, he's being sued by his mailman who broke his arm when he slipped on his porch. He goes to the bar and gets drunk as a skunk, all the while bitching about lawyers. The bartender even adds his lawyer story since he's being sued by a guy who crashed his car on the way home a month earlier. The guy stands up and shouts, "All lawyers are assholes!" A guy in the back says, "You better take that back or I'm gonna kick your ass!" The man asks, "Why? Are you a lawyer?" He says, "No! I'm an asshole!"

*   *   *

A pirate goes into the pub with his ships steering wheel on his willy. The bartender asked him, “Why?” He said, "Ahrr, It drives me nuts!"

*   *   *

A new businessman buys a saloon back in the old wild west. The place is hopping on opening night. People are drinking, dancing, gambling, and fighting. His business venture is off to a great start until some dude runs in the door and yells, "Head to the hills! Big Dave’s a comin!" The whole place empties out in the blink of an eye. The place falls silent as he stands behind the bar all by his lonesome. Soon, a shadow casts over the building. In through the swinging doors ducks the biggest man he's ever seen in his life. He must be seven feet tall and weigh five hundred pounds. He walks up to the bar with a frightening stare from yellow eyes. "Whiskey!" his voice booms. The proprietors knees are knocking so hard you could here them from Texas. His hands are shaking so bad he could barely hold the bottle still enough to open it. The giant snatches the bottle out of his hands, bites the neck off the bottle, chews the glass and downs the whole contents. "Dddoo do yyou wwwwhanttt aaanother?" stuttered the barkeep. "Ain't got no time." he replied. Big Dave’s coming!"

*   *   *

A guy hears a load knock on his front door at three o’clock in the morning. When he asks, “Who’s there?” The response was a very slurred, “Can you give me a hand? I need a push.” “No! Go away!” When he returns to bed his wife asked him what was going on. “Oh, it’s just some drunk wanting me to go outside at three in the morning in the pouring rain and give him a push." His wife says, I can't believe your not going to help him. Remember, it was just last month that we got a push from that nice man when we broke down. God loves drunks too you know." Now he's got the guilt trip so he puts his shoes and coat on and steps out into the rain. "You still out here?" "Yeah." "Do you still need a push?" "Yes please." "Where are you?" The drunk answers, "I'm over here. On the swing."

*　　　　　*　　　　　*

A drunk falls off his barstool down at the local watering hole. He tries to stand up but can only manage to pull himself along the floor to get outside. He's hoping the fresh air will help him stand, but to no avail. He crawls all the way home. He pulls himself up to unlock his front door as quietly as possible trying not to wake his wife. He slides inside and crawls up the stairs and into his bedroom. He quietly undresses and slips into bed and breaths a sigh of relief when his wife doesn't even stir.

The next morning he wakes up with his wife screaming at him, "You sorry son of a bitch! You got drunk at that bar again didn't you? I told you not to go down to there anymore because you always drink way too much!" He was baffled that she even found out. "How did you know? I was so quiet coming home." She said, "The bartender called. You left your wheelchair there again!"

*　　　　　*　　　　　*

A drunk goes up to the bartender and asks if he wants to make a bet. "I'll bet you a hundred dollars that if you slide a shot glass down the bar, I can piss in it without spilling a drop." The bartender laughed and said, "You're on!" The guy climbs up on the bar and drops his pants. The bartender slides the shot glass down the bar and the drunk pisses all over the place. He barely managed to get one drop in the glass. The bartender is laughing at him and says, "Man, that was the easiest hundred bucks I ever made." The drunk is laughing as he gets down off the bar. The bartender asks why he's laughing. He says, "Because I bet my friend over there a grand that I could piss all over your bar and make you happy about it."

* * *

Ray went to meet his friend at a bar. His friend shows up late with a red face and his clothes all disheveled. "Where the hell have you been?" "Oh man! I got here a half hour ago, met a girl and ended up taking her out to the dark alley and took her to pound town in the back of my car." "Really? Just like that?" "Yeah! She's a whore! I didn't even buy her a drink, she was just ready to go. The slut is still out there. If you want, I'll watch your drink and you can go get some ass too."

Ray goes out to the dark alley and finds his friend's car. She pulled him into the back seat and they start going at it. Just then, a cop rolls through and shines his spotlight into the car. "Hey! What's going on in there?" Thinking quickly, Ray said, "It's okay officer, it's my wife." "I'm sorry, I didn't know." Ray replied, "Me neither, till you turned that damn light on!"

* * *

A guy hooked up with a girl named Betty in a bar and they go out to his car and start fooling around in the back seat. After he penetrates her he says, "Sorry babe, if I'd known that you were still a virgin I would have taken more time with you." Betty said, "If I knew you had more time, I would have taken my pantyhose off."

*   *   *

Three pieces of rope are out on the town and are going from bar to bar getting kicked out of every establishment for being drunk and rowdy. They go into one bar and after a few rounds start getting unruly and are asked to leave. This is the last bar in the area so they decide to sneak back in. They try the back door. Locked. They come up with a plan. One sneak in and then unlock the back door for the others. One of them puts on some sunglasses as a disguise and tries to walk in. Again, he's recognized and gets told to leave. Another tries a hat. No dice. They have one more shot at this to keep partying. The third messes up his hair really good and twists himself up in a bow. He goes up to the bartender and asks for a drink. "Aren't you one of the same pieces of rope that we just kicked out?" He replied, "Nope. I'm a frayed knot."

*   *   *

A guy is sitting at the bar, nursing a beer and the peanuts in the bowl start talking to him. "That's a really nice tie you got there, it goes great with your eyes. Did you just get a haircut? It looks great. That sure is a handsome suit you're wearing." The guy calls to the bartender, "What's the deal with these nuts?" "Oh," the bartender says.
"They're complimentary."

*   *   *

A drunk slurs well enough to ask directions to the bar's bathroom. After a few minutes there's a loud scream. The bartender goes back, knocks on the door and asks the drunk if he's okay. The drunk is crying in pain saying that something in the toilet bit his balls and won't let go. The bartender barges in and says, "You idiot!
You just flushed the mop bucket!"

*   *   *

A pirate comes into a bar with a parrot on his shoulder, patch on his eye, a wooden peg leg and has a hook for a hand. A guy notices but needs a few drinks to get the courage to finally ask him, "How did you lose your hand?" "Arr!" says the pirate. "We were invading another vessel and some swabbie chopped it off with his cutlas sword!" "Ouch!" The man continues; "How did you lose your leg?" "Arr! I got washed overboard and before me mates could pull me back aboard, a shark took it." "Ow!" sympathizes the drunk. "How did you lose your eye?" "Arr!" says the pirate. "Seagull shit!" "Wait. What? How can you lose an eye from seagull shit?" The pirate explained, "T'was me first day with the hook!"

*   *   *

A cop is cruising by a bar right before closing time when he sees a guy fall out of the front door. He pulls over across the street and just watches this guy try to stand up and struggle to make it to the parking lot. The cop is laughing to himself and can't wait for the guy to get behind the wheel so he can bust him. The guy gets up but immediately falls over again. People are leaving the bar and stepping over the drunk on the sidewalk. The guy makes his way to the parking lot and drops his keys. He bends over to pick them up and kicks them instead. He bangs his head on the side of a car when he tries to pick them up again. The cop is sitting in his car laughing out loud now. He lets the rest of the bar patrons drive right on by. The drunk finds his keys and stabs them at a car door for two minutes before he realizes that it's the wrong car. The bar is closed and everyone is gone by the time this guy gets in his car and finally pulls out of the parking lot. The cop lets him get down the block before he pulls the guy over.

The cop asks the guy to get out of his car and walk a strait line while his dashboard camera films it. The guy does the test without a problem. He's asked to put his head back and touch his nose. He does it without trouble. After that he recites the alphabet backwards. The cop is annoyed and makes him blow into the breath analyzer. It reads all zeros. "I don't understand! How can this be? You were just falling down intoxicated a minute ago. How can you be perfectly sober now?" "Easy," the guy explains.
"I'm the designated drunk!"

* * *

You know you've had too much to drink when you feel something cold brush against your shoulder. When you turn around, it's the sidewalk.

* * *

Three guys, Bobby, Pete and Mike meet up in the pub for the first time in the new year and start talking about the great New Years Eve party that they went to last month. Then they started discussing and eventually arguing about who drank the most. "I got more drunk than anyone," said Bobby. "I missed midnight and spent the whole night blowing chunks." "That's nothing!" said Pete. "The last I remember is being chased out of my house naked by what I thought was my wife, hitting me with a shoe. I was all the way down the street when I realized I was on the wrong block." Mike says, "I got you both beat! I got a D.W.I.
I woke up in jail with used rubbers in my pocket and some guy's name tattooed on my chest and I don't remember a thing." "Yeah. You got us both beat," Pete said.
Bobby disagreed, "No, you guys don't understand!
Chunks is my dog!"

BLONDES
(DoDiDo)

*   *   *

A naked blonde walked into a bar with a poodle under one arm and a two foot salami under the other. The bartender said, "What is this? A joke?"

*   *   *

A guy tells the bartender, "Man, I got a great blonde joke for you." The bartender stops him. "Wait a minute buddy. Before I was bald I had a full head of blonde hair. You see that blonde guy over there? He's an all-state kickboxing champion and my blonde waitress is a power lifting champ. Do you still want to tell a blonde joke now?"
"Nah," the guy says. "I don't want to explain it three times."

*   *   *

A blonde's neighbor is doing yard work and keeps noticing her running out of the house to the mailbox. After the tenth time he finally asked what she was doing.
Her response was, "My computer must be broken. It keeps telling me I have mail."

*   *   *

The blonde was desperately looking for a date for the New Years party. Her friends wondered why. She said, “Because in 2012, every SINGLE person will die.”

*   *   *

A blonde was in a delicatessen waiting to be served. The owner gives out scratch-off tickets to the people in line to keep them occupied. The blonde scratches hers and starts shouting, "I won a motor home! I won a motor home!" Everyone in line gets excited for her. The owner asks, "What are you talking about? You didn't win a motor home. Lady, the best thing we're giving away is a coffee maker!" She's still adamant that she won a motor home. He takes the ticket from her and points out what it really says. "WIN A BAGLE!"

*   *   *

The pilot's voice came over the intercom. "Ladies and gentlemen, this is your captain speaking. That loud noise you just heard was one of our engines going out. Please don't worry, we have three perfectly good engines. However, our scheduled landing time will be delayed by about a half an hour. Sorry for any inconvenience." A few minutes later there was another loud bang. "Ladies and gentlemen, this is your captain again. It seems that we have just lost another engine. Not to worry though, we still have two others that will get us to our destination safely but our landing time will be delayed by another half hour. Your air hostess will be providing complimentary drinks shortly." After ten more minutes another loud bang rocked the cabin. "Ladies and gentlemen, this is your captain again. We just lost our third engine but this plane is perfectly capable of flying on one engine. However, we will have to push back our estimated time of arrival just a little bit more. We apologize for any inconvenience this may have caused." A blonde lady said to man sitting next to her, "If that last engine goes out; we're going to be up here all night."

*   *   *

A blonde, a brunette and a redhead were walking through the desert. They all carried one item with them. The brunette brought a big jug of vitamin water for when she got thirsty. The redhead had a watermelon in case she got thirsty or hungry. The blonde was carrying a car door.
“Why?” others asked. She explained,
“Hello! It’s the desert! If I get hot, I can just roll down the window!"

*   *   *

A blonde takes a couple of vacation days from work and decides to treat herself to a new haircut and dye job. As a brunette she's feeling pretty smart. She goes for a drive out to the country with the top down enjoying the day. She sees a field filled with grazing lambs. She pulls over to the farmer on the side of the road and asks him, "If I can guess how many lambs you have, can I have one? I've always wanted a lamb." The farmer smiles, looks across the field full of lambs and says, "Good luck." The new brunette guesses, "Three hundred forty six." The farmer is shocked that she got it right. He keeps his end of the deal and lets her pick one. She puts it in the back of her convertible and starts to drive off. The farmer stops her and says, "Ma-am, if I guess what color your hair really is, can I have my dog back?"

*   *   *

Did you hear about the skeleton that was found in the back of the closet with long blonde hair?

She was the 1995 Hide and go seek champion.

*   *   *

A blonde chick driving along, gets pulled over for speeding. A blonde, female, cop asked her for her drivers license. "I don't think I have one." "Sure you do," says the cop. "It's probably in your purse." As she's looking in her purse the cop continues, "It's about the size of a playing card and it has your picture on it." The blonde pulls out her compact mirror and hands it to the officer. "Is this it?" The police woman looks at it and says, "You can go. I didn't know you were a cop too!"

*   *   *

A girl finds her blonde friend standing at the kitchen table looking frustrated. "What's wrong?" "I've been working on this tiger puzzle all day. I can't get any of these pieces to fit." Her friend says, "You Dingbat! That's a box of Frosted Flakes!"

*   *   *

Why don't blondes eat M&Ms?

They're too hard to peel.

*   *   *

How do you know if a blonde has been using your computer?

There is white-out all over your screen.

*   *   *

How are blondes like turtles?

Once they're on their backs they're screwed.

*   *   *

How many blondes does it take to screw in a light bulb?

Blondes don't screw in light bulbs. They screw in hot tubs.

*   *   *

Why don't blondes go ice fishing?

They'll drown trying to fry their catch.

*   *   *

Why don't blondes play water polo?

They're afraid the horses will drown.

*   *   *

A blonde walking alongside a creek looks across and sees another blonde. "How do I get on the other side?" Her reply was, "You silly goose, you are on the other side!"

*   *   *

A blonde accidentally ran over her cat's tail with the lawnmower. She immediately took her beloved pet to Walmart because it's the worlds largest retailer.

*   *   *

A blonde goes into a bank with a big bag full of cash and a deposit slip. The bank manager asked, "Did you horde all this cash yourself?" The blonde said,
"Nah! My sister horde half of it."

*   *   *

A blonde got a job in the factory where they are still making Tickle me Elmo dolls. The foreman shows the cutie around and informs her of her duties at the end of the assembly line. The line has to be shut down repeatedly so they can wait for the blonde to catch up. The foreman gets annoyed because of the work stoppage. He goes out to see what was the matter. He sees the blonde franticly sewing bags of nuts to the dolls as they came to her. The foreman shouted, "You dummy!
I said give each one Two Test Tickles!"

*   *   *

What do blondes and pianos have in common?

Once they're no longer upright, they're Grand.

*   *   *

Two blondes were sitting in an Oklahoma park talking. One asked the other, “Which do you think is farther away...Florida or the moon?” The other blonde turns and says, “Hellooooo, can you see Florida?”

*   *   *

Three blondes and three brunettes were applying for the same job with the phone company. The foreman put them to the test. "Whichever team can put the most telephone poles in the ground before five o'clock will get the job." At the end of the day they all returned to his office dirty and exhausted. The foreman asked the brunettes how many poles they installed. They told him, "Eight." "Wow! That's pretty good." When he asked the blondes, they said, "Two." "That's it? The brunettes put in eight." "Yeah, we saw their work," said the blondes. "Did you see how much they left sticking out of the ground?"

*   *   *

A blonde complains to the doctor that her body hurts everywhere she touches. She pushed her finger into her shoulder to show him and cried out in pain. She touched her elbow and screamed. She pushed on her knee and then her ankle and screamed again and again.
The doctor told her, “Your finger is broken.”

*   *   *

Tracy, a blonde, was playing Trivial Pursuit with her friends. She rolled the dice and landed on Science & Nature. Her question was, “If you are in a vacuum and someone calls your name, can you hear it?” Tracy thought for a moment then asked, “Is it on or off?”

*		*		*

A ship's captain found a stowaway aboard his vessel. He asked the young blonde woman what she was doing. She apologized to the Captain and explained that the first mate was letting her stay onboard and was bringing her food and water in exchange for sex everyday. The Captain asked where she was going. She said she didn't care, she just wanted to see the world. The Captain said, "You nitwit! This is the Staten Island ferry!"

*		*		*

Six blondes walk into a bar shouting, "Fifty seven days! Fifty seven days!" They order three pitchers of beer and carry on shouting. Three more blondes walk in and join them shouting, "Fifty seven days! Fifty seven days!" They're all high fiveing and whooping it up. Two more blondes come in and start chest bumping the rest while chanting, "Fifty seven days! Fifty seven days!"

The bartender brings them a few more pitchers and some more glasses but has to ask them, "What's going on?" They all were so excited to tell him, "We all did a puzzle together. On the side of the box it said 'Three to five years.' We did it in just fifty seven days!"

*		*		*

Did you hear about the blonde that tried to swim across the English channel?

She got half way when she realized she couldn't make it. So she swam back.

*   *   *

Dawn was visiting her blonde friend, Linda, who just acquired two new dogs. “Their names are Rolex and Timex.” Dawn asked, “Why would you name them that?” Linda said, “Hello! Because they’re watch dogs!”

*   *   *

How many blondes does it take to change a light bulb?

Two. One to hold the diet Coke and one to call Daddy.

*   *   *

A blonde thinks her boyfriend is cheating on her. She buys a gun and goes to teach him a lesson. She goes to his apartment and finds him in the arms of another woman. She puts the gun to her own head and begins to cry. Her boyfriend shouts, “No Honey! Don’t do it!” She says, “Shut up jerk! You’re next!

*   *   *

Scott went to the nude beach for the first time and met a blonde and blue hottie named Brandy. After frolicking in the sand and sun all day Scott realized that he had gotten badly sunburned. EVERYWHERE! Brandy invited Scott back to her place for some after-sun aloe application. Of coarse she volunteered to rub him down and it ended up with them having repeated, vigorous fornication. Scott's dick felt like it was on fire. He went into her kitchen looking for some relief. He poured himself a tall glass of milk and submerged his burning member into it. Brandy walked in and squealed, "So that's how you guys load that thing!"

MOB

(You talkin to me?)

*　　　　*　　　　*

A mob extortionist is feeling the heat from the cops and decides he needs to lay low for a while. To make the collections from the neighborhood businesses he hired a deaf mute. He figured a mute won't be able to talk to the cops if he gets caught.

A month passed and the mob guy comes back with an interpreter and asked the mute with sign language; "Where's the money?" The mute hands him an envelope with twenty grand in it. The mob guy tells the interpreter to ask him, "Where's the rest of the money?" The interpreter signs to him and the mute signs back,"That's all of it." The mob guy gets his response from the interpreter and pulls out his pistol and puts it to mute's head and tells the interpreter to ask him again, "Where's the rest of the fifty grand?" The mute right away starts signing like crazy. "Okay! Okay! It's in the tree stump on the left side of the Central Park entrance on 57th street." "What did he say?" The interpreter says, "He said he still doesn't know what your taking about and you don't have the balls to pull that trigger."

*　　　　*　　　　*

A mob guy is walking home from the lounge with his dame one night. They pass by a jewelry store and she says, "Oh Franky, look at those earrings! They're beautiful!" The mob guy takes a brick and throws it through the window and grabs the earrings for her. "Thanks Franky." They pass a clothing store and she sees a fur coat. "Oh Franky, look at that beautiful coat. I would look great in that!" He throws a brick through that window and grabs her the coat. They walk on and come across a shoe store. "Oh Franky, look at those gorgeous shoes! They would go great with my new coat!" He says, "Doll face! Do you think I'm made of bricks?"

* * *

Grampa wrote a letter to Louie in prison. “My tomato garden is going to be hard to dig up by myself. I wish you were here to help me like always.” Louie wrote his Grandpa back, “No Papi. Don’t dig up the garden. That’s where I buried the bodies. I wish I could help. I’ll be out in a few years though.” The next morning the F.B.I. came and dug up the whole garden only to leave disappointed. The next day a letter arrived from Louie, “Papi, that’s the best I could do. You can plant your tomatoes now.”

* * *

A wiseguy and his best girl are walking down 6th avenue in New York when she spots a big ring in a window. "Ew! Lenny that ring is gorgeous!" "C'mon doll-face. I'll get you that ring." They go into the store and she's ecstatic when she puts it on. However, it doesn’t fit. Lenny writes a big check out to the jewelry store and tells them he will pick it up on Monday. When Lenny returns on Monday the jewelry shop owner informs him apologetically that his check bounced. Lenny replied, "I know. I just came by to tell you I had a GREAT weekend!"

*　　　　　*　　　　　*

Tony 'Knuckles' goes to church. He asked the priest for the Lord's help. "With what can our Lord help you with?"
"It's my hearing, father. I'm really worried."
The priest asks him to bow his head. The priest puts his hand on Tony's head and says a short prayer. The priest asks, "Now, is your hearing any better?"
Tony says, "I don't know father. It's not till Wednesday."

MAKE BELIEVE

(Fairy Tales)

*　　　　　*　　　　　*

Two women sitting quietly, minding their own business.....

*　　　　　*　　　　　*

What did Cinderella say when she got to the ball?

Ugumggffff!

*　　　　　*　　　　　*

What did Batman say to Robin right before they got in the Batmobile?

"Robin, just get in the fuckin car!"

*   *   *

Gippetto and Pinnochio were sitting around the toy shop. Gippetto told Pinnocio that he was a man now and it was time to move on and find his own place, maybe start a family. He doesn't see Pinnochio again for months until one day Pinnochio returns to town. "Pinnochio, my boy! How's it going? How's things with the women?" Pinnochio explains that he and his girlfriend are having problems in bed because of splinters. Gippeto tells him he has the solution and hands him a sheet of sandpaper. Months go by and they run into each other again. "Pinnochio! My boy! How are you?" "How's things going with the women?" Pinnochio says, "Women? "Pfft! Who needs women?"

*   *   *

Saddam Hussein was walking through the Iraqi desert after the allied forces just whipped the Iraqi army's ass. He was pissing and moaning and cursing America under his breath while kicking his own destroyed tank parts. He kicked a brass lantern and a Genie appeared with a cloud of smoke. The Genie granted him one wish in return for freeing him from a thousand years of captivity. Saddam was ecstatic. He pulled out a map of the middle east from his shirt pocket and told the Genie that he wants the whole area to be under his rule. The Genie looked at his map and scoffed. "I'm sorry, but this is a very tall order. This is out of my power. It can't be done. "Saddam was now livid. "You said anything I wanted!" "I'm sorry, it's too much." Saddam recoiled to his second dream, "How about making the Houston Texans Super bowl champions?" The Genie thought for a second and said, "Let me see that map again."

*   *   *

Superman was very bored one day. He was flying around in disbelief that there was no crime or wrongdoings going on anywhere in the world. While flying across the ocean he looked down and saw Wonder-woman lying on an island shore naked. He flew by a little closer and saw that she looked horny and was undulating her hips with her eyes closed. Superman thought about going down there and seeing if she was interested in fooling around. Then he figured that since he was the fastest man in the world, he could just fly down there, screw her and fly off before she even knew what happened.

He flew around again, zoomed down at mach speed, nails her hard and fast and takes off again. Wonder-woman abruptly sat up. "What was that?" The Invisible man rolled off of her and cried, "I don't know but it hurt like hell!"

*   *   *

What's the difference between a northern fairy tale and a southern fairy tale?

The northern fairy tale begins, “Once upon a time.” The southern fairy tale starts, “Y’all aint gonna believe this shit!”

*   *   *

Mickey Mouse and Minnie are getting a divorce. The judge calls Mickey up to the sidebar and tells him, "You know Mickey, I don't think you have good enough grounds to divorce Minnie just because you think she's a little crazy." Mickey said, "I didn't say I thought she was a little crazy.
I said she was fucking Goofy!"

*   *   *

What goes hippity click, hippity click, hippity click?

The Easter bunny with polio.

*   *   *

Why does the Easter bunny hide eggs?

So nobody would know he's been screwing chickens.

*   *   *

The Lone Ranger gets captured by the Indians. They are going to burn him at the stake at sunrise. The Lone Ranger whispers in his trusty horse Silvers' ear. The horse turns and leaves in a flash. He returns a few hours later with a beautiful young woman. The Lone Ranger takes the woman into his holding tent and ravishes her. He steps out, whistles for his horse again and whispers in his ear again, "I said POSSE you stupid ass! Go get the POSSE!"

*   *   *

Chris walked into the local bar and sees Jamie, and his head is shrunken to the size of a baseball. He sees a guy sitting at the piano playing a Billy Joel tune and he's only twelve inches tall. Chris asked Jamie, "What's up with your head?" "Oh, Myles and I got a genie out of that lantern we found. He granted me two wishes and Myles got one. I told him I just wanted a little head. Then he misunderstood again when I asked for a twelve inch penis. Instead I got a foot tall pianist." Chris said, "That sucks. Where's Myles?" "He's dead. He said he always wanted to be hung like a black guy."

*   *   *

A guy in the midst of a bitter divorce finds a bottle at the beach. He wipes it off and a Genie appears. "I have been enslaved in this bottle for a thousand years. For my freedom I'll grant you three wishes. But, whatever you ask for, your wife will get twice as much." "I want a million dollars," the man says quickly. "It is done. Your wife will get two million dollars." "I want a brand new yacht." "Done. Your wife will get two new yachts." The guy said, "Okay, now I wish to be beaten half to death!"

*   *   *

Why don't witches wear panties?

So they can get a good grip on the broom.

*   *   *

Why doesn't Santa Clause have children of his own?

He can only come once a year.

*   *   *

Little Red Riding Hood was walking to Grandma's house when out from the bushes sprang the Big Bad Wolf. "I've been waiting to screw you!" Little Red Riding Hood pulled out her Colt .45 and said, "Bullshit! You're going to EAT ME like the story says!"

*   *   *

Cinderella was disappointed that she couldn't go to the Ball. Her stepmother and stepsisters left her with all the chores to do while they went without her. She sat scrubbing the floors and sobbing. All of a sudden 'POOF'! Her Fairy God Mother arrived out of thin air and introduced herself. "Why are you so sad?" she asked. "Everyone went to the Prince's Ball without me. I have to stay home and do work." The Fairy God Mother waved her magic wand and 'POOF!' The house was clean. She then turned a small pumpkin into a ticket to the Ball for her. "But I don't have transportation," said Cinderella. ‘POOF!’ With the wave of her wand, turned another pumpkin into a beautiful horse drawn carriage. "That's really nice, but I don't have anything to wear." The Fairy God Mother waved her magic wand again and a stunning white gown appeared on Cinderella complete with glass slippers. "It's all so nice, except..." "Except what dear?" asked the Fairy God Mother. "Well... I'm having my period right now and I’d hate to ruin this dress.” The Fairy God Mother waved her wand once more and turned another pumpkin into the most absorbent tampon in all the land. Off Cinderella went to the Ball with the warning that she had to be back by midnight because the spell will wear off and everything will turn back into a pumpkin.

Midnight passed and Cinderella had not returned. One o'clock turned, then two, then three. No Cinderella. Finally at four fifteen Cinderella stumbled through the door, ragged, shoeless and exhausted. "Where have you been?" inquired her Fairy God Mother. "I met the most wonderful man in the world. He was charming and handsome and just perfect. I think I'm in love." "Oh. So you and the Prince hit it off huh?" Cinderella said, "No, not the Prince! His name is Peter Peter!"

MIDGETS
(A little funny)

* * *

What do you call a midget fortune teller that escaped from prison?

Small, medium at large.

* * *

A midget is angry about the horrible service and goes to complain to the restaurant manager. "I'm not happy you know!"
The manager replied, "Which one are you?"

* * *

A midget complains to the doctor about his balls hurting every time it rains. The doctor tells him to come back next time he feels discomfort down there. The next rainy day he returns and tells the doctor how bad it hurts. The doctor tells him to hop up on the examining table, lay back and relax. The doctor then takes a pair of scissors and starts cutting around the bothersome area. When he's done he asks the little fellow to hop down and see how it feels. The midget hops down and walks in a circle and exclaims that it doesn't hurt anymore. "What did you do? It feels fine now." The doctor said, "I just cut a couple of inches off of the top of your goulashes."

*   *   *

What's red and has seven dents in it?

Snow White's cherry.

*   *   *

Why do little people hate to use tampons?

They keep tripping over the string.

*   *   *

Two midgets go out on the town, partying and spending their yearly work bonuses. They get wasted while bar hopping. They pick up a couple of hookers and go back to the motel room. After some more drinking and a little dancing the lights go out and they retreat to separate beds. One midget has a whiskey dick and can't get it up. He can hear his buddy through the darkness, "1,2,3 UGH! 1,2,3 UGH!" "Damn!" He struggles to get it erect but has no luck. His friend can be heard across the dark room getting louder and faster, "1,2,3 UGH! 1,2,3 UGH! 1,2,3 UGH!" He has the girl try to fluff him up but to no avail. Dejected, he just goes to sleep.

They wake up the next morning, the girls are gone and they have wicked hangovers. One midget asked the other, "How did it go last night?" "Oh, it sucked! I was so drunk, I couldn't get my dick hard. It was like shooting pool with a rope." His friend says, "You think that's bad?
I couldn't even get on the bed!"

* * *

A midget is on an elevator when a big, black guy gets on. The little guy is in amazement of how large this man is. He clumsily stammered, "How big are you?"
The black guy towering over him replies, "I'm six foot eleven. I weigh three hundred and eighty pounds. Name's Turner Brown." He extends his hand for the greeting.
The midget's eyes roll back into his head and he passes out. When he comes to, the black guy is standing over him asking if he was okay. The little guy opens his eyes, sees him and scrambles to the corner. "What happened?" The black guy tells him, "You asked me how big I am and when I told you, you fainted." "What did you say again?" He repeated, "I'm six foot eleven, I weigh three hundred and eighty pounds. My name is Turner Brown." The midget gets up, brushing himself off and says, "Oh! Your name is Turner Brown? Man, I thought you said turn around!"

LEPERS
(Ew!)

* * *

What did the Leper say to the hooker when he was done with her?

You can keep the tip.

* * *

How does every sporting event begin in the Leper colony?

Everyone takes their face off.

*   *   *

How do lepers make spaghetti?

Hit another leper with a tennis racket.

*   *   *

How do you know the letter is from a leper?

There's a tongue stuck to the envelope.

*   *   *

What do you call a leper in a jacuzzi?

Stew.

*   *   *

A leper in a bar gets pissed at the drunk for laughing at him.
The drunk says, "I'm not laughing at you. The guy behind you is dipping his chips in your shoulder."

*   *   *

How do you know when a Leper has been using your shower?

Your soap got bigger.

OLD PEOPLE
(But goodies)

*　　　　*　　　　*

An old couple that sleep in separate beds get frisky after coming home from the oyster bar. He invites his wife of sixty years over to his bed. She slowly gets out out of her bed and trips on her robe and falls. The husband quickly helps her up. "Oh sweetie pie. Did my little pumpkin wumpkin hurt her hiney winey?" He helps her into his bed and slowly screws her. Afterwards, she's going back to her bed and trips and falls again. He goes, "Clumsy whore!"

*　　　　*　　　　*

An old lady was lifting her glasses up and down on her eyes in front of the A.T.M. trying to read her bank statement. As I approached, she asked if I wouldn't mind helping her check her balance...
So I pushed her over.

*　　　　*　　　　*

An old couple is sitting down for dinner on their anniversary when the wife suggests that they should make this a little more romantic. He agrees. He lights some candles. "Remember how we used dine in the nude? We should do that again." "Fine," he says. They both disrobe and continue having dinner. "Honey," she says. "My nipples are just as hot for you now as when we first got married." He replied, "That's because they're in your soup!"

*   *   *

A priest goes to visit an elderly parishioner who hasn't been to church in a few weeks to make sure she's okay. She invites him in and explains that she hasn't been feeling well. She asks him to have a seat while she gets some tea. The priest notices a bowl of nuts on the coffee table and helps himself to one since he hasn't eaten lunch yet. That one becomes two, then three, and before he knows it, the whole bowl is empty. Just then the old lady comes out of the kitchen and the priest immediately apologizes for eating all her nuts. "That's okay dear. I just suck the chocolate off them anyway."

*   *   *

What do old people taste like?

Depends.

*   *   *

A wealthy, old man gets himself a trophy wife. A smoking hot, gold digging, twenty six year old. A real life Barbie doll. On their wedding night, it's time to consummate the marriage. The young woman who knows she's about to be set up for life from his will, plans on giving him a heart attack tonight. She appears from the bathroom wearing high heels, fishnet stockings, and a black lace teddy. She sees him with a huge erection, a nose clip and he's twisting in some ear plugs. "What are you doing?" she asks nervously. "Well honey," he begins. "There's something about me you must know. There are two things I CAN'T STAND!... The sound of a woman screaming and the smell of burning rubber!"

*   *   *

A couple on their fiftieth wedding anniversary go for a drink at the local pub. “Remember the first time we came here and had sex against the fence out back?” he asked. “Lets go try that again.” His bride blushes but agrees. The bartender overhears this and follows them around back to see if these old people can really pull this off. They hobble over to the fence hand in hand with their canes in the other hand. She pulls up her dress and he leans her up against the fence. They immediately start having the fastest and most frantic sex anyone’s ever seen. Screaming and crying out for two blurring minutes before they fall to the ground exhausted. They stand up, put themselves back together and start walking back inside. The bartender tells them, “That was really impressive. You must have a great sex life together. What’s your secret?” Still shaking, the old man replies, “Fifty years ago that wasn’t an electric fence.”

*   *   *

On their sixtieth wedding anniversary the wife goes to the boutique to buy herself some nice lingerie. The girl working there helps her overcome her embarrassment and explains that the higher quality the item is, the more sheer the fabric. She notices the price tag and is shocked at the expense of this stuff that is practically invisible. Her husband's eyesight is not that good anymore, so she figures why spend the money. I can just tell him I'm wearing nice lingerie and he won't notice the difference. She goes home with an empty box and tells her husband she has a surprise for him. She goes into the bedroom and comes out totally naked. "What do you think of this new lingerie?" He says, "For that kind of money, they could have at least ironed it for you!"

* * *

A guy is shopping the bread isle in a supermarket when a cute employee asked if he would like some assistance. "I'm looking for some raisin bread," replied the man. "Oh, it's up on the top shelf. I'll get a ladder." As she walked away to get a ladder he noticed her short skirt. When she returned he positioned himself to hold the ladder steady and to give himself the best view. She climbed the ladder and handed him the loaf of raisin bread on her way down. "I'll take two please." She climbed back up giving him another good look. When she got back down there was another gentleman there and he too asked for some raisin bread. They both held the ladder for her. When she looked down there was now an old man looking up at her. "Is it raisin for you too sir?" He said, "No, but it's twitching a bit."

* * *

Billy was visiting his father at the nursing home and noticed his Pop kept leaning over the side of his chair. As they are talking a nurse kept coming over to sit his father upright. This happens repeatedly throughout the conversation. Billy is becoming concerned about his Dad's mental state. "So Dad, how do you like it here?" His Father replied, "It's okay. But they never let me fart!"

* * *

A bored, young, hot shot lawyer decided to mess with the old man sitting next to him on the plane. "Would you like to play a game?" The old man was trying to take a nap. "No thanks. I just need forty winks." "Come on. It'll be fun," he persisted. "I'll ask you a question and if you get it wrong or don't know, you pay me five dollars. Then you ask me a question. If I don't know I'll pay you fifty dollars." The old man is intrigued and consents to play. The lawyer begins, "What is the distance between the sun and the moon?" The old man reaches into his pocket and gives him five dollars. The old man asks, "What goes up hill with three legs and comes down with four?"

The lawyer gets out his laptop and starts looking for an answer. He even e-mails all his smart friends and coworkers. After an hour he wakes up the old man, counts out the fifty dollars and hands it to him. The old man pockets the money and starts to go back to sleep. The lawyer shakes him awake and asks, "What goes up hill with three legs and comes down with four?" The old man reaches into his pocket and hands the lawyer another five and goes back to sleep.

* * *

Three old men are sitting around the recreation center at the retirement home complaining about this and that. One old man says, "When I wake up I go to the bathroom and it takes about five minutes just to get out a dribble of piss." The second old man says, "When I get up I sit on the toilet and I'm there straining for an hour before I can have a bowel movement, and it's just a little bit." The third guy says, "Every morning I take a wonderful piss at seven and a nice, big, healthy shit at eight." His friends say, "That sounds great! Why do you sound like you're complaining?" He says, "I don't wake up till nine."

* * *

An old man and his girlfriend are sitting outside the retirement home looking at the lake talking about the things in life that they miss most. She says, "I miss dancing." He says, "I miss sex. Would you mind holding my penis for a while?" She says, "Are you kidding me? You couldn't get it up if you had a helium pump." "I know," he says. "But it would be nice if you just held it for me." She complies and they both think it's nice. They make it a date to do it every night after dinner.

One night, he's not at the meeting spot so she goes looking for him. After checking the dinning room and the recreation center, she finally finds him in another woman's room and she's holding his penis. "Are you cheating on me? We had such a nice thing going. How could you?"
He says, "She has Parkinson's!"

*　　　*　　　*

A group of 40 year old friends plan a reunion and they decide to have it a restaurant named Tony Tabuka's because they have pretty waitresses in tight skirts and low cut blouses. When they're 50 they have their party at Tony Tabuka's because they have a great wine selection. At 60 they choose to go back there because the food is good and healthy. When they are 70 they return to Tony Tabuka's because it has wheelchair access. When they are 80 the decide on Tony Tabuka's because they've never been there before.

*　　　*　　　*

An old man goes to church with his wife for the first time in many years. During the sermon he hands his wife a note that reads, "I just let out a silent fart, what should I do?" His wife hands him a note back that said, "Change the batteries in your hearing aid."

*   *   *

What’s the best part about being over one hundred years old?

No peer pressure.

*   *   *

What's the best thing about having Alzheimer's?

You get to hide your own Easter eggs.

*   *   *

Nancy goes to visit her father in the nursing home. While they were talking, the nurse comes in and gives her dad a pill and a cup of water to wash it down. As the nurse is walking out, Nancy asked her what that pill was. "Viagra," the nurse answered. "Viagra? He's ninety five years old! Why would you give him Viagra?" The nurse said, "It keeps him from rolling out of bed."

*   *   *

Two old couples were playing bridge when the women go into the kitchen to make coffee. The men are talking about restaurants in the area. Rob asked, "Frank, I know your memory is not that great but what was the name of that place you two went to on your anniversary?" Frank thought for a minute. "I can't recall. What is the name of the red flower that people like?" Rob guesses, "A rose?" "Yeah! That's it!" He then calls into the kitchen, "Hey Rose! What was the name of that restaurant we went to last night?"

*   *   *

A woman calls her elderly mom's cell phone. "Be really careful on the highway. I just heard on the news that there is some maniac out there driving the wrong way." Her mom says, "There's not just one. There's hundreds of them!"

*   *   *

An old couple at the nursing home get some quiet time together after dinner. They sneak into the woman's room and help each other get undressed. He asked, "Is there anything you would like me to do for you?" She answered shyly, "I would love to be licked down there." He kisses his way down her body but comes up quickly. "It smells terrible down there!" "Oh, that must be my arthritis," she said.
"In your vagina?" "No. It's in my shoulders. I can't wipe my ass."

*   *   *

Two old men were sitting on a park bench and one of them tells the other his birthday is tomorrow. "I bet you can't guess how old I'll be." His friend says, "Stand up and pull your pants down and I'll be able to tell." "I can't do that. We're in a park." "Just do it!" He pulls his pants down. "Now pull down your poo poo undies." "Come on. We're out in public. There's people..." Just pull them down," his friend encourages. He does it. "Now, stick your middle finger up your ass." What? There's kids right over there." "I'll be able to tell how old you are if you do it." He licks his finger and sticks it up there. His friend says, "You're ninety five." "Oh my gosh! How could you tell my age by me sticking my finger up my ass?" His friend said, "You told me this morning."

WACKED
(Out there)

*   *   *

Terry was walking past a mental health hospital on her way to meet a friend for lunch. As she walked along the wooden fence she can hear someone with dain bramage on the other side yelling, "13,13,13,13". She stopped to look through a knothole and they stabbed her in the eye with a pen. As she held her eye and reeled in pain she could hear, "14,14,14,14."

*   *   *

Two patients in a mental hospital, Patrick and Ray Ray, whom the doctors call 'Nuck n Futz,' were walking around the grounds enjoying the day. Ray Ray went over to the pool and jumped in. Still wearing his robe, he quickly sank to the bottom. Patrick stood and stared at his friend in the deep end. After a minute he jumped in and pulled him out. The hospital curator witnessed the whole seen. He went to Patrick's room the next morning and told him that he has good news and bad news. "The good news is; after reviewing your records and witnessing your acts of heroics, you are fully capable of returning to the outside world. The bad news is; your friend Ray Ray committed suicide last night. He hung himself with the belt from his robe."
Patrick said, "He didn't kill himself. I hung him up to dry."

*   *   *

A guy says to his psychiatrist, "I can't help but think I'm invisible. People always ignore me."

The shrink said, "Next!"

*   *   *

A guy says to his psychiatrist, "I can't stand this! Some days I think I'm a teepee and some days I think I'm a wigwam."

The shrink says, "I know what you're problem is. You're too tents."

*   *   *

What's better than winning a gold medal at the Special olympics?

Not being retarded.

*   *   *

A drunk, a heavy smoker and a sex addict all die and go to heaven. St. Peter tells them that God has a message for them. "Go back and live your lives. Only healthy from now on. As soon as you slip up and go back to your vices you're coming right back here." 'POOF!' They're back on earth. They all agree to straighten up their act. As they're walking home, they pass by a bar and the drunk says he's going in for a drink. The other two beg, "No, don't drink. You'll die!" He apologized, but said he needs a Scotch. He flicked his cigarette on the sidewalk and went in for his last beer. The sex addict warned the smoker, "You pick that up, we're all dead."

*   *   *

What has a million legs and can't walk?

Jerry's kids.

*   *   *

A guy goes to the shrink and explains to him that he's really stressed out at work and is cursing a lot.
The psychiatrist asked, "What seems to be the problem?"
He answered, "I JUST FUCKING TOLD YOU JACKASS!"

*   *   *

How do you get a clown to quit smiling?

Smash his face with an axe.

*   *   *

What should you do if you're attacked by clowns?

Go for the juggler.

*   *   *

Why shouldn't you go down on a clown?

They taste funny.

*   *   *

Why did Princess Diana cross the road?

She wasn't wearing a seat belt.

*   *   *

Sherlock Holmes and Mr. Watson were walking through the park when they came across three women sitting on a park bench eating bananas. "Good afternoon ladies," Sherlock said with a tip of his hat. "Do you know them?" Watson asked. "Are you referring to the nun, the prostitute and the housewife? No, I don't know them." "Then how are you aware of their occupations?" inquired Mr. Watson. "Elementary my dear Watson. The nun was the one cutting up her banana into slices. The prostitute ate her banana with one bite. The housewife was holding the banana with one hand and forcing her head down onto it with the other.

*   *   *

A fat guy is walking out of a Stop-N-Rob store with four hot dogs, six candy bars, popcorn, two bags of chips and a big gulp soda. A homeless guy sitting against the wall said, "Sir, I haven't eaten in three days." The fat guy replied, "Man, I wish I had your willpower!"

*   *   *

Some neighborhood kids knock on the door of a kid who doesn't have any arms or legs. His mother answers the door. The kids ask her if he could come out to join them for a baseball game. The mom says, "Now, you all know that Billy has no limbs. How do think he could possibly play baseball with you?" "Oh, we don't need him to play, we want to use him for second base."

*   *   *

A masochist begs to the sadist, “Beat me, whip me, make it hurt!”
The sadist simply says, “No!”

*　　　　　*　　　　　*

A couple was fooling around in the back of his van. She starts getting kinky and told him to spank her. He complies. Then she starts screaming, "Whip me! Whip me!" He starts franticly looking around for something to use since he doesn't have a belt. He thinks outside the box and snaps off the van's antenna. He whips her ass good and they have a great climax. A week later her wounds start to fester. The doctor told her, "You just contracted a raging case of van-aerial disease."

*　　　　　*　　　　　*

A big burley biker was riding his Harley across the Golden gate bridge when he saw a girl going to jump off. "What are you doing?" he asked. "I'm going to commit suicide." She was very pretty so the biker asked if he could get a kiss first. "Sure, why not?" She gave him the most warm, soft, wet, loving kiss he's ever had. "Wow!" he said. "That was the best kiss ever! You could sell those and make a fortune. Why would someone like you want to commit suicide?" She replied, "Because my parents hate when I dress like a girl."

*　　　　　*　　　　　*

Three guys' car break down in front of a farm house in the middle of nowhere. They ask the farmer if they can spend the night. "Okay," he says. "But stay away from my beautiful daughters." They all have to sleep in the same bed. When they wake up, the first guy says, "Wow! I had an amazing dream about getting a hand job from one of the farmers daughters." Another guy says, "Hey, I had the same dream. It was a great hand job." The guy in the middle says, "Not me! I dreamt I was skiing."

*　　　　*　　　　*

Jimmy, while visiting Spain, goes to Pamplona and takes in a bull fight. After the fight he goes across the street to a restaurant for a meal. He can't help but notice the plate of food on the table next to his. He calls the waiter over and asked what those two big round things were on that man's plate. "Those are cohones. They're the bull's balls from the fight. They're our specialty. If you come again tomorrow, come early if you want them." The next night Jimmy returns early and orders the cohones. The waiter returns with his plate, but the balls are far smaller than what he saw last night. He stops the waiter before he walked away and asked why. The waiter told him, "Senior, the bull doesn't always lose."

*　　　　*　　　　*

Tom, an average guy, gets shipwrecked on a deserted island with Jennifer Anniston. After a few months of surviving on fish, coconuts and bananas they where both really bored. Jennifer was missing her fast paced life and was starting to get horny. She decides to give the guy a treat and goes into his makeshift hut completely naked.

Tom was shocked and very excited. They screwed all morning. He put a pause on the action to ask her for a favor. "Sure," she says. "Anything, just keep doing me!" "Alright," Tom says. "Just please put on my pants and shirt." The starlit found this odd but wanted more sex so she agreed. "Now, put on my shoes and coat." After she does, he looks her up and down and asks her to wear his hat. He steps back for another look. He grabs a small piece of burnt wood from the fire and uses the ash to draw a mustache on her. "Would you mind if I call you Bob?" he asks. "I guess that would be alright," she says frowning. Tom says, "Hey Bob, you'll never guess who I'm fucking."

*   *   *

Why don't blind people skydive?

Nobody wants to hear a German Shepherd scream from ten thousand feet.

*   *   *

At a Science Expo, the judges make their way to an exhibit that boast multiple flavored fruit. Examples include oranges that taste like oranges on first bite but taste like watermelon when you get to the inside. Bananas that taste like pineapples when you get to the bottom. Also, there are papayas that tastes like grapefruit and peaches and pears that taste like kiwi and strawberries. The judges are amazed but inquire about the apples. "Oh, that's the highlight of our experiment," the young botanist says. "They taste like pussy." "That's great!" one judge says. "I love pussy!" He bites into the apple, winces, then spits it out in disgust. "This tastes like shit!" The kid says, "Turn it around."

*   *   *

A hotel patron asked the receptionist, “Can all the porn in my room be disabled?” The clerk barked, “You sick freak! You'll watch the normal porn like everyone else!”

*   *   *

How do you make a dead baby float?

Add a scoop of ice cream and some root beer.

*   *   *

What's the world's most effective pick-up line?

Does this rag smell like chloroform?

*   *   *

Steve was jogging down the beach and came across a girl with no arms and no legs lying on the sand crying. "What's the matter?" he asks. "Well I guess I'm just feeling sorry for myself. I've never been hugged before." So, Steve picked her up, gave her a big hug. He put her down after she stopped crying and he carried on jogging feeling good about his kind deed. The next day he jogs by and sees that she's crying again. "Now what's up?" "I've never been kissed before," she says. Feeling sorry for the poor girl since she has no limbs, he picked her up and gave her a kiss. She stopped crying, he put her down and jogged off. The next day she's in the same spot crying her eyes out. "Now what's wrong?" Steve asked. She pathetically says, "I've never been screwed before." So he picked her up and threw her in the ocean.

*   *   *

A woman goes to her doctor complaining of stomach cramps. The doctor examines her and says, "Your going to have to get use to long sleepless nights full of crying and diaper changing." She says, "Why? Am I pregnant?" He says, "No. You have bowel cancer."

*   *   *

A guy was limping down the street dragging his bad leg behind him. He sees another guy walking towards him dragging the same leg. His first thought was that the guy was making fun of him and he started to get mad. Then he began to wonder if the guy had the same injury. As they passed one another the guy grabbed his bum leg and said, "Vietnam. '68." The other guy pointed behind him and said, "Dog shit! Half block back!"

*   *   *

What's the difference between your pregnant girlfriend and a light bulb?

You can unscrew a light bulb.

*   *   *

How is locking your keys in your car like getting a girl pregnant?

Both problems can be solved with a coat hanger.

*   *   *

What's twelve inches long and makes a woman moan all night?

Sudden Infant Death syndrome.

HELEN KELLER
(What?)

*   *   *

How did Helen Keller burn the side of her face?

She answered the iron.

*   *   *

How did she burn the other side?

They called back.

*   *   *

How did Helen Keller burn her fingers?

Reading the waffle iron.

*   *   *

How did Helen Keller's parents punish her?

They left the plunger in the toilet.

They also told her to read the stucco walls.

*   *   *

What was Helen Kellers worst Christmas gift?

A Rubicks cube.

*   *   *

Why did Helen Keller masturbate with only one hand?

She needed the other hand to moan.

*   *   *

Why was Helen Keller's leg yellow?

Her dog was blind too.

*   *   *

Why did Helen Keller's dog run away?

You would too if your name was Aaaurrrhuuhhh.

*   *   *

Why couldn't Helen Keller drive?

She was a woman.

DOCTORS

(Rectum? Damn near killed him!)

*   *   *

A guy waiting in line at the unemployment line New York notices a sign advertising a job for a gynecologist assistant. The man inquires about the job when it's his turn. The clerk informs him the job entails helping the women off with their clothes, cleaning the area for examination and helping them change positions if needed. "That sounds great!" says the guy. "Where do I sign up?" "In Boston," says the clerk. "That's okay. I don't mind relocating." "No, the job is only two blocks from here. The line starts in Boston."

*   *   *

A guy cuts off all ten of his fingers trying to fix the lawn mower. He makes his way to the hospital and the doctors scolds the young man. “Why didn’t you bring your fingers? We could have sewn them back on and you’d be good as knew.” The guy replies, “I couldn’t pick them up.”

*   *   *

A beautiful blonde goes to the gynecologist. She has her feet up in the stirrups when the doctor asked her if she's ever been numb down there. She said she hasn't, so the doctor put his face down there and went, "Numb, numb, numb!”

*　　　　　　*　　　　　　*

Gynecologist: "Man; you have a big pussy!" "Man; you have a big pussy!"
Woman: "You didn't have to say it twice!"
Gynecologist: "I didn't."

*　　　　　　*　　　　　　*

A woman getting ready for her gynecological appointment trimmed her pubic region and got very carried away. She shaved it all off. She wanted to check out her handy work in the mirror but couldn't get a good angle to see. She took the mirror off the wall and put it on the living room floor. She was straddled over the mirror when her husband walked in. He shouted, "WHOA! Watch out for that hole! You could break your leg in that thing!"

*　　　　　　*　　　　　　*

A woman goes to the doctor complaining that she got stung by a bee while golfing.
The doctor asked, "Where did you get stung?" She said, "Between the first and second hole." The doctor said, "There's your problem. Your stance is too wide."

*　　　　　　*　　　　　　*

A local yokel goes to the country doctor with a really bad cough. The doctor can't find any cough syrup to give him so he loads the guy up with laxatives and sends him on his way. The nurse asked what good the laxatives will do. The doctor said, “In a half hour he'll be too scared to cough.”

*   *   *

Patient: "Doctor, kiss me! Kiss me! Please!"
Doctor: "No! I can't. It's against my hippocratic oath. I probably shouldn't even be screwing you!"

*   *   *

A woman tells her gynecologist that she got her pocket vibrator stuck and could use a little help. The doctor puts her legs up in the stirrups to have a look. "It's way up there! I don't know how on earth I'm going to get that out." The patient says, "I don't want it out! Just change the damn batteries!"

*   *   *

A gynecologist asks his patient, "Have you ever had a check up here before?"
The woman said, "No, but I've had a couple of Germans, a Russian and a Pollock."

*   *   *

A guy gets told by his doctor that there is good news and bad news. "I'll take the bad news first." The doctor says, "Okay. Well, I'm sorry to inform you that you have cancer and you probably only have six months to live." "Oh my God!" says the guy. "That's terrible! What's the good news then?" The doctor asks, "Did you see my new red headed receptionist when you came in?" "Yeah," proclaims the man. "She's hot!" The doctor said, "I'm fucking her."

*   *   *

A lady gets the bad news from her doctor;
Doctor: "You have cancer AND you have Alzheimer's."
Lady: "Oh no! Well, at least I don't have cancer."

*   *   *

A guy whose elbow is bothering him goes into the supermarket to look for some pain pills. He asks the pharmacist for some guidance. The pharmacist tells him about their new machine that can get to the bottom of it. The guy checks it out. It cost a dollar and requires a urine sample. The guy goes into the bathroom with the supplied cup, fills it, and tips the contents in the machine's opening and inserts a dollar. The machine starts whirring and shaking. The lights flash and a bell rings indicating the results were ready. The guy reads the provided result card..."You have tennis elbow. Rub Hydrocortisone on the area three times daily." The guy buys some Hydrocortisone and starts driving home.

On the way home he starts getting pissed off about how the machines are taking over the world and it's probably full of shit anyway. "What the hell does a machine know about tennis elbow anyhow?" He decides to mess with it. He went home, got some of his wife's urine, some from his son and daughter, he jerked off into the cup and then threw some of his dog's shit into mix. He went back to the store with a smirk on his face, poured the concoction into the machine and payed his dollar. The machine started to rattle and shake, the lights went crazy and smoke came out of the back. "Here are your results," read the card: "Your wife is cheating on you and she has an S.T.D. Your daughter is pregnant. Your son has a raging cocaine habit. You're feeding your dog too much wet dog food and now it has worms. If you don't stop masturbating, your tennis elbow is never going to get better!"

*   *   *

A woman goes to the pediatrician with a baby who just won't eat. The doctor examines the malnourished kid and asked the woman if he is breast fed or bottle fed. "Oh, he's breast fed," she says. The doctor gently squeezes the woman's breast and lightly pinches her nipples. The doctor says, "Your breasts are all dried up. There's no milk in there." The woman says, "I know. I'm his grandmother! But I'm glad I came."

*   *   *

What do you call a gynecologist in Florida?

The spreader of old wives' tails.

*   *   *

A guy goes back into his doctors office to hear the results of the barrage of tests he's been taking all morning. The doctor told him to sit down. He then informed him that he has terminal cancer. The guy, as you can imagine, starts to have a meltdown. The doctor does his best to console him but the guy is coming unglued, crying uncontrollably. The doctor, looking at his watch, tells the guy that he has a tee time in a half hour and invites him to join him on the golf coarse and unwind a bit before returning to work.

While out on the golf course the guy runs into some of his friends and they ask him what's wrong because he doesn't seem like himself. "Well, this is my doctor and he just told me that I'm dying of Aids." His friends are shocked. They buy him a drink and give their condolences before going on to play their game. The doctor pulls the man aside and says, "You are dying of CANCER. I didn't say anything about you having Aids." "I know," says the guy. "I just don't want any of them fucking my wife when I'm gone!"

*   *   *

A male nurse was giving a sponge bath to a female patient that's been in a coma for almost a year when her brain wave monitor showed heightened activity. The doctors down the hall noticed the alerts and came rushing in to ask the nurse what he had done. "I don't know, I was just washing between her legs when she started to twitch." The doctors agreed amongst themselves that maybe sexual stimulation might get her out of her comatose state. They asked the nurse if he wouldn't mind having sex with someone in a vegetative state in the name of science. He agreed to it.

The doctors left him to it and went down the hall to watch the monitors from the nurses station. They saw almost immediate improvement of her brain waves and her heart rate steadily improved until it started to race. Then suddenly it flat lined. The doctors ran down the hall and into the woman's room and asked the nurse as he was pulling his pants back up. "What happened?" "I don't know," he replied. "I guess she choked!"

*   *   *

Cliff has an early morning dentist appointment. His wife, knowing how much he hates the dentist, decides to wake him up nicely so his day is not so bad. They played around and end up finishing in a 69. Now he's running late. He quickly brushes his teeth and gets dressed. He noticed that he can still taste his wife. He brushed his teeth again and rinsed with mouthwash. On the way there he's eating mints like crazy. He gets to the dentist and they lay him back in the chair and right away the dentist says, "You got into a 69 with your wife before you came in here didn't you?" "Oh God! You can smell her on my breath, huh?" "No," the dentist says. "You got shit on your forehead."

*   *   *

A doctor tries to explain to a man that his wife's test results were inconclusive but the results were narrowed down to two things: It was either Aids or Alzheimer's.
"What should I do?" he asks the doctor. "Relax," the doctor begins. "As you're driving home, make three consecutive lefts and then kick her out of the car." "What good would that do?" the man asks. The doctor says, "If she finds her way home, don't fuck her."

*   *   *

Pete goes into the doctors office and tells the doc that his problem is really embarrassing. The doctor reassures him that he's a professional and he need not worry. "I've been doing this for thirty years you're not going to show me anything I haven't seen before." Pete nervously begins to undo his pants and pulls them down to reveal the smallest penis the doctor's ever seen in his life. It's no bigger than a peanut. The doctor starts laughing uncontrollably. It takes him a few minutes to regain his composure. After wiping the tears from his eyes he apologizes to his patient. "I'm sorry Pete, that was very unprofessional of me. I don't know what came over me. Now, what seems to be the problem?" Pete says, "It's swollen!"

*   *   *

Mr. Brown goes to the doctor complaining of an orange penis. The doctor examines him and they run all the tests imaginable. All the tests come back negative. The doctor starts asking him more questions. "Are you using new chemicals at work?" "No." "Did you start a new diet?" "No." "Do have any new hobbies?" "Nope." "What do you do in your spare time?" the doctor asked. "Nothing much. Just sit around, eat Cheetos and watch porn."

*   *   *

A guy runs up to the E.R. surgeon, "I heard about the accident! Is my wife okay?" The doctor sits the man down and explains that she is paralyzed from the neck down. "She's never going to be able to do anything for herself again. You are going to have to feed her, dress her, bathe her, even change her colostomy bag." "Oh my God! That's terrible! That's the worst thing I've ever heard!" The doctor then says, "I'm just fucking with you! She's dead!"

*   *   *

An artist has all his work in a gallery. He goes back a week later to check on how things are going and notices all his paintings are gone. The proprietor tells him that they were all sold to one person. "A wealthy man came in just yesterday and was asking questions about you and he wanted to know if the value of paintings go up after the artist death. I told him they did and he bought them all." "Who was this guy?" asked the artist. "Your doctor."

*   *   *

Katy goes back to the doctor complaining about the side effects from the testosterone shot. "I've started to grow hair in weird places." "Like where?" the doctor inquired.
Katy replied, "My nuts."

*   *   *

A doctor tells his patient after the examination, "Your dying and you don't have much time." "That's terrible! How long do I have?" The doctor says, "Ten." "Ten? Ten what? Months? Weeks?" The doctor says, "9, 8, 7, 6,...."

*   *   *

A woman goes to the eye doctor complaining of seeing spots. The receptionist asked, “Have you ever seen a doctor?” The woman says, “No. Just spots.”

*   *   *

A wealthy benefactor is touring her donated hospital wing with the chief surgeon. They pass by one room and she notices a patient masturbating furiously in his bed. "What in the world is that man doing?" she asked. The surgeon told her that the man has 'Testiculitis' and he has to relieve the pressure twice a day or his testicles will explode. As they pass another room there is a patient getting a blow job from a pretty nurse. "What's going on here?" The surgeon replied, "Same deal, better insurance."

*   *   *

A really old lady goes to a gynecologist for the first time because her vagina itches. The doctor takes a quick look and determines that she has crabs and starts to write a prescription for some cream. The old woman argues that she does not have crabs. "Don't worry. There's nothing to be embarrassed about, lots of people get crabs," says the doctor. "I can assure you that I am not one of those people," she insists. The doctor tries again to reassure her. "It's no big deal, you just rub some ointment on the area and they go away in no time." The women again insists that she does not have crabs because she is still a virgin. The doctor is taken aback and goes in for a closer look at the problem area. "You're right!" he says apologetically. "They're not crabs. They're fruit flies. Your cherry's rotten!"

POLITICAL
(Incorrectness)

*   *   *

Chelsea Clinton was getting nervous before her wedding and was asking her mom about her honeymoon. Hillary asked her if she's ever had sex before. Chelsea said, "Not according to Dad!"

*   *   *

What's the difference between God and Obama?

God doesn't think he's Obama.

*   *   *

What do God and Obama have in common?

Neither has a birth certificate.

*   *   *

Did you hear that the Washington D.C. Zoo got a new African lion?

The White house got a lying African.

*   *   *

Obama was visiting Israel to discuss world peace and find some economic solutions for America's woes. On his second day he was touring the West bank and was killed by sniper fire. The Israelis offered to prep his body and ship him back for five hundred thousand dollars. Or keep him there for burial for the low price of four hundred bucks. The American diplomats discuss the dilemma at length over dinner and tell the Israelis that they better have him shipped back to America. "But you have money problems as it is. Why not bury him here?" The Americans said, "Because the last time you people buried someone important, he came back three days later."

*   *   *

If opposite of PRO is CON...

The opposite of Progress must be Congress.

*   *   *

What did Lee Harvey Oswald say to Larry Bird and Michael Jordan?

Through the book depository window, across the grassy knoll, nothing but neck!

*   *   *

A mugger jumped out of the alley. “Give me your money!” “But I'm a congressman,” cried the man. The mugger said, “In that case, give me MY money!”

REDNECKS
(All Y'all)

*　　　　*　　　　*

How do you know when a redneck is married?

He has tobacco spit down both sides of his truck.

*　　　　*　　　　*

How does a hillbilly mother know her daughter is having her period?

Her son's dick taste like blood.

*　　　　*　　　　*

How do we know that the toothbrush was invented in Arkansas?

If it came from anywhere else it would be called a teethbrush.

*　　　　*　　　　*

What's the difference between Mexicans and rednecks?

Mexicans grow, mow and blow.
Rednecks just fiddle, whittle and diddle.

*   *   *

What do call a redneck girl that can outrun her brothers?

A virgin.

*   *   *

How many country singers does it take to change a light bulb?

Five. One to actually change the bulb and four to sing about how much they miss the old one.

*   *   *

How many rednecks does it take to eat a squirrel?

Three. One to eat it. The other two watch for cars.

*   *   *

Boudrouex: "What's the fastest way to get to Baton Rogue?"
Tibidouex: "You walking or driving?"
Boudrouex: "I'm driving."
Tibidouex : "That's the fastest way."

*   *   *

A redneck called down to the front desk of an Alabama hotel. "I gotta leak in my sink."
They replied, "Go ahead."

*   *   *

Emma Sue passed away and Billy Bob called 911. “We’ll be out your way shortly. Where do you live?” Billy Bob replied, “Eucalyptus drive.” The operator asked, “Can you spell that?” There was a long pause. “How ‘bout I drag her over to Oak street? Y’all can pick her up there.”

*   *   *

A gas station in rural Georgia was advertising, ‘Free Sex with Fill-up.’ A redneck pulled in, got a fill-up and asked about free sex. The proprietor said, “Pick a number between one and ten. If you get it right, you get free sex.” Bubba guessed, “Four.” “Nope. You were close. It was Three.” Bubba came back for another fill-up the next week. He asked about free sex. “Guess the right number then.” Bubba guessed, “Nine,” “Nope. It was eight. You were close though.” Bubba got back in his truck and said to his buddy Billy Ray, “I think this free sex game is rigged.” Billy Ray responded, “My ass it’s rigged! My wife won five times this month!”

*   *   *

Mark was applying for the sheriff department in small town in south Texas. The Sheriff told him that all his qualifications were great and it was just the attitude suitability test that was left. He then slid a service weapon across the desk and asked Mark to go out and kill a meth dealer, two illegal aliens, three muslim extremest, Jessie Jackson, Al Sharpton and a rabbit. Mark asked, "Why the rabbit?" "Congratulations! You have the right attitude! When can you start?"

MILITARY

(Ooo Rah!)

*　　　　*　　　　*

A guy who stutters real bad joins the army and gets accepted into the airborne division. On the day of their first real jump their instructor goes over their instructions one last time while in the plane. "Okay men, after you jump out you're going to count to ten, pull your ripcord, your parachute will open and float you safely down to the drop zone. Find the truck number that corresponds with your squadron number, secure your chute, get in the back of the truck and we will all meet back at the base for chow. Does anyone have any questions?" The stutterer slowly raises his hand. "What is your question?" barks the instructor. "S s s sa Sssargent? Huh h h, How hhhigh ddddid did y, ya, yah, you ssss say we we we were ssssssupposed tt to, How high ddddid yy you sss say we were ss supposed ttt to cccc ca count up to?" The instructor looked at him curiously and said, "You better count to ONE!"

*　　　　*　　　　*

A grizzled old Marine was having a drink at the bar. A drunk young lady came up and teasingly asked him if he ever smiled. "When was the the last time you got laid?" He thought for a second and said, "1955." "Wow! That was a long time ago! You poor guy. Why I don't take care of your manly needs?" They go into the ladies room for a bit and when they come back to finish their drinks she asked, "How where you able to last so long if it's been that long since you had sex?" He said, "It hasn't been that long. It's only 2130 now."

*   *   *

Two Air force pilots were having a drink in the Officers club. One was an F-15 plot the other was a F-16 pilot. They began arguing over which aircraft was better. Anything you can do I can do better, etc. They decided to settle it the next day. The F-16 pilot takes the lead and starts doing barrel rolls, loop de loops and inverted dives. The F-15 pilot is working hard to keep up with him and his tight turns but stays with him. The F-15 pilot takes the lead and punches his duel engine machine to fly mach 3 straight up to the heavens. The single engine plane struggles to keep up with that power but is not far behind. After a few other tests they both come to the conclusion that they are pretty evenly matched. The F-15 pilot says, "Okay, one more test. I know you can't copy this!" The F-16 pilot says, "I can do anything you can!" He says, "Oh yeah? I'm killing one engine and going home."

*   *   *

A man in the Navy is out at sea for the first time and asks another sailor what they do without women during these long stretches. "Oh, we just use that barrel with the hole in it." After a couple of nights at sea the sailor gives it a whirl. It feels great! He comes back night after night until one night he sticks his willy in and nothing happens. He asks the first mate about it and the first mate informs him, "It's your turn to be in the barrel!"

*   *   *

An Air Force captain asked an airman if he had change of a dollar for the vending machine. “Sure buddy,” was his reponse. “Is that anyway to address an officer? Let’s try that again. Airman! Do you have change of a dollar?” He replied, “No sir!”

*   *   *

Little Johnny's all grown up and signs on the dotted line at the Navy recruiter's office. "What made you join the Navy son?" "My father said it would be a good idea." "Your father's very wise. What does he do?" Johnny replied, "He's in the Army."

*   *   *

First sergeants from the Army, Navy, Air force and Marines were arguing in the mess hall over whose troops have the biggest balls. The argument gets pretty heated when they decide to settle it out on the field. They go out to the Marine proving ground and watch the Marines crawling under barbed wire with machine gun fire whizzing over their heads. The Marine gunny sergeant yells to one, "Marine, stand up and come here!" "Sir! Yes sir!" He stands up and gets mowed down by the bullets. "You see? My troops are fearless. Nothing but balls!" The others are not impressed. They go to the ship yard and the Navy first sergeant yells at one of his troops on the bow of an aircraft carrier, "Sailor! Jump in there and bring me up that anchor!" The sailor does a pretty swan dive in but nothing comes up but his last bubbles. "You see? The Navy has the balls." They all climb aboard a C-130 gun ship with the Rangers. The back door lowers and the Army first shirt tells the platoon leader to give up his parachute and get out. He follows orders. "You see gentlemen? Without hesitation. All balls!" The plane lands at Dover Air Force base. When they step out they notice a mechanic working on the tail section of a big C-5 cargo plane. "Airman!" "Yes sir?" "Jump!" "FUCK YOU!!!"
"You see?" says the first shirt. "THAT troop has balls!"

*   *   *

At a morning war briefing it was brought to the Presidents Bush's attention that over in Iraq three Brazilian soldiers were killed in a fire fight. George Bush asked his advisor, "How many is a brazilian?"

*   *   *

A limousine pulled up to a military base's checkpoint with a four star general in the back. "Sorry, but I can't let you through without a window sticker," said the guard. The general told his driver to proceed. "Sir! I can't grant you access, you'll have to turn around." The general again instructed the driver to proceed. The sentry asked the general, "Sir, I'm kind of new. Do I shoot you or the driver?"

*   *   *

A guy goes into a bar and starts downing shots of Bourbon like water. One after another, ordering three at a time until the bartender begs him to slow down and explain what's troubling him. "Well," says the guy. "I'm Army Airborne and today was my first jump." "Congratulations! Here's one on the house. But why does it seem like you're trying to kill yourself?" "Well, all through boot camp and ground training and even jump school I was head of my squadron. When it got time to make our first real jump I was supposed to lead my troops out of the plane. I got to the door and froze. It's a big difference from the practice platform back on base. My drill instructor told me to get to the back of the line and build my courage. After I watched all my comrades jump, I got to the door and I froze again. "What happened then?" asked the barkeep. "Well my D.I. stood behind me and told me that if I didn't jump he was going to fuck me in the ass." "Holy shit! Did you jump?" The soldier replied,
"A little at first."

GAMBLING
(Crap!)

*   *   *

What has six balls and screws you twice a week?

The lottery.

*   *   *

The lottery:
An extra state tax for people who are bad at math.

*   *   *

I won the Polish Lottery.

A dollar a year for a million years.

*   *   *

A guy bursts in his front door all excited. "Honey, I won the lottery! Pack your bags!" His wife asks, "What should I pack? For the tropics or the Alps?" He said, "I don't care, just get out!"

*   *   *

A bum asked a passerby for a dollar. "Are you going to get a drink with it?" "No sir. I don't drink." "Are you going to gamble it away?" "No sir. I don't gamble either." "Then can you come home with me so I can show my wife what happens to someone that doesn't drink or gamble?"

*   *   *

A man is suddenly woken out of a dead sleep by a voice screaming in his head. "GO TO VEGAS!" It really rattled him. As he was eating breakfast he heard that voice in his head again. "TAKE ALL YOUR MONEY AND GO TO VEGAS!" Whoa. That was weird, he thought. As he was driving to work, he heard it again. "SELL ALL YOUR STUFF, TAKE YOUR MONEY AND GO TO VEGAS!" He tried to shake it off. It happened a couple more times throughout his work day. "SELL ALL YOUR STUFF, TAKE YOUR MONEY AND GO TO VEGAS!" He could barely concentrate on his work. As he was driving home the voice was steady screaming at him to go to Las Vegas. He was starting to freak out a little. He's never even been to Vegas. He tried to get some rest that night but the voice wouldn't let him. "SELL ALL YOUR SHIT! TAKE YOUR MONEY! GO TO VEGAS!" It said it over and over.

The next morning he takes all his things of value to the pawn shop, gets a fist full of cash and heads to the airport. He tried to get some rest on the plane since now the voice has stopped. The plane lands and he's wandering around the airport feeling like a fool until the voice chimes in his head again. "Get a cab and go to the Bellagio." He gets out at the Bellagio and the voice tells him, "Go down to the casino." He walks down to the casino and the voice says, "Go strait to the roulette table." He looks up at the roulette table, and it has what seems like a guiding light from above. The crowd just parts for him. He gets to the table and the voice says, "Put all your money on black 19!" The man is just shaking. He finally realizes that THIS is his calling. It's like an epiphany. THIS IS IT! With trembling hands he puts all his money on BLACK 19. The wheel spins and the ball drops. RED 22. He hears the voice in his head again, "Shit!"

GAY
(Not that there's anything wrong with that.)

*   *   *

Beauty is in the hole of the behinder.

*   *   *

What does GAY stand for?

Got Aids Yet.

*   *   *

What does AIDS stand for?

Another Infected Dick Sucker.

*   *   *

What do you feed a gay horse?

Haaaaaaay.

*   *   *

How do you separate the men from the boys in San Francisco?

With a crowbar.

*   *   *

What are the 3 most commonly used pick up lines in gay bars?

Mind if I push your stool in?
There's a party in my mouth. You coming?
Your face or mine?

*   *   *

What's the most sung song in a gay karaoke bar?

Don't you make my brown eye blue.

*   *   *

How did Rock Hudson die?

He had Neighbors up his ass.

*   *   *

How did Jim Neighbors die?

He took a dip in the Hudson.

*   *   *

Two gay hitchhikers get picked up by a big rig driver. During the drive, one of the passengers lets out a squeaky fart and they both start giggling. A few minutes later the other pushes out a high pitch toot. They both start giggling again. The burly truck driver says, "You guys are too light in the loafers. Let me show you how a real man farts." He lifts his leg and cranks out a booming dose of flatulence. The two gay guys start laughing uncontrollably. The truck driver asks them why they're laughing. They both squeal in unison, "HE'S STILL A VIRGIN!!!"

* * *

Lezbi friends and go homo!

* * *

What did one lesbian frog say to the other?

Hey; we DO taste like chicken!

* * *

What do you call lesbian twins?

Lick a likes.

* * *

How do lesbians hold their liquor?

By the ears.

* * *

How can you you tell you're in a lesbian bar?

Even the pool table doesn't have any balls.

*　　　　*　　　　*

What do you call it when you mix fifty lesbians and fifty postal workers?

One hundred people that don't do dick.

*　　　　*　　　　*

If a gay guy and a lesbian share an apartment and they both get evicted, who moves out first?

The gay guy. He's already got his shit packed!

*　　　　*　　　　*

What do you call the bouncer at the Shove it Inn?
A flame thrower.

*　　　　*　　　　*

Wendle moves out to the country to get away from it all. While sitting on his front porch enjoying the peace and quiet with a cup of coffee he sees a trail of dust being kicked up by an old Chevy truck heading up his driveway. This good old boy gets out, "Morning neighbor! I just wanted to swing by and welcome you to the area. I'm having a party tonight at my place and I would love it if you came by." "Sure," says the new guy. "What's going on?" "Oh, it's going to be great! There's going to be lots of drinking, some dancing, a little fighting and a ton of fucking." "Sounds great. How many people are going?" "Oh, it's just me and you!"

*   *   *

How do you get a gay guy to screw a girl?

Shit in her snatch.

*   *   *

Two gay guys walking down the street and one of them has a midget under his arm.
He says to his friend, "You want a hit off this before I throw him away?"

*   *   *

A farmer brings home a new stud rooster for the hen house. The new rooster struts in to find an older rooster already in there and he's filled with apathy. "Look," the older rooster begins, "This is MY house and these are MY hens. You can just turn around and go back where you came from!" The new rooster is not leaving quietly after seeing all those beautiful chicks around. "How bout YOU leave old cock? This is a job for a young cock a doodle to do." "Tell you what," says the old rooster. "Lets race for it. Twice around the barn. Whoever wins, gets to stay and the loser leaves." "Okay old man, you're on. But I'm telling you there's now way you can beat me. I'll even give you a head start."
On your mark..." With that, the old rooster took off out of the hen house and around the barn. He was just passing the farmers porch to begin his second lap, the younger rooster was gaining on him; BLAM!!! The farmer slaughtered the new rooster with his shotgun. Blew him to bits. "Damn!" said the farmer. "That's the third gay rooster I bought this month."

*   *   *

Did you know that there were gay dinosaurs?

They were called the Megasoreass.

*   *   *

Did you know that there were lesbian dinosaurs too?

The Eatalotopus.

*   *   *

Pat runs into his old friend Ray at the local watering hole. Pat asked, "Where've you been? I haven't seen you in a long time." Ray told him, "I've been going to school at night. I'm taking a course in Logical Deductions." Pat's lost. "Deductions? What is that? Like math?" Ray replied, "No. It teaches you to come to conclusions about things faster." Pat was still confused. Ray gave him an example: "Do you have a lawnmower?" Pat says, "Yeah." "Well," Ray continued, "You're probably a heterosexual. You have a yard right?" "Yeah," Pat said frowning. "So," Ray concluded, "If you have a yard, that means that you probably have a house. And if you have a house, that means that you probably have a family in it. Wife and kids?" "Yeah, so?" asked Pat. "Therefore, you're a heterosexual." Now Pat gets it! "That's pretty cool!" Ray finished his beer and headed home.

Pat is dying to share his newfound knowledge with someone. After a few more drinks he finally asked the bartender. "Wanna hear something cool?" "Sure. What's up?" "You got a lawnmower?" Pat asked smugly. "No," the bartender replied. Pat said, "Faggot!"

*   *   *

Did you know Pocahontas's brother was gay?

His name was Pokeahiney.

*   *   *

How do gays fake orgasms?

They spit on your back.

*   *   *

Did you hear about the lesbian sorority?

Bi Ate a Pie.

*   *   *

What do you call a male interior designer?

A back splasher.

*   *   *

A newly out lesbian comes home from college and is helping Mom cook dinner. Mom, who is stirring the pot of stew asks, “So you lick women down below?” Nervously she answers, “Yes.” Her mother points the wooden spoon at her and shouts, “Don’t you EVER complain about my cooking again!”

*   *   *

What's the difference between a fag and a fridge?

A fridge doesn't fart when you pull your meat out.

*   *   *

What's invisible and smells like semen?

Fag farts.

*   *   *

An employment office is holding interviews. The first guy comes in and says his name is McCoy. “What did you do at your last job Mr. McCoy?” asked the interviewer. “I was a cork socker.” “What’s a cork socker?” “Well I worked at a winery and I put the corks in the full bottles and used a mallet to sock them in.” “Oh, okay. We’ll give you a call if anything comes available.”

The next guy comes in and says his name is McCoy too. “Really? Well, what did you do at your last job Mr. McCoy?” “I was a sock tucker.” “What’s a sock tucker?” “I worked in the garment industry and I tucked socks in sets of three into a plastic package for sale.” “Oh, well we’ll give you a call if something comes up.”

The next guy comes in and says his name is McCoy. “Are you kidding me?” asked the interviewer. “The last two guys that were in here were both name McCoy. One was a cork socker and the other was a sock tucker. What’s your story?” With his hand on his hip and a very effeminate voice he says, “Well, I’m the REAL McCoy!”

*   *   *

How do you get four queers on a bar stool?

Turn it over.

*   *   *

A lesbian asked the sex shop clerk, “Where are the vibrators?” The woman gestures with her finger, “Come this way.” The lesbian says, “If I could come that way, I wouldn’t need a vibrator.”

*   *   *

Two gay guys walk past the morgue. One of them says, "You wanna stop in here and suck down a couple of cold ones?"

*   *   *

Four gay guys kicking back in the hot tub. A wad of cum floats to the surface.
"Alright, who farted?"

*   *   *

Two gay guys went to the carnival. One wants to ride the Merry-Go-Round but the other is too scared. "Fine! I'll just go by myself!" He jumps off the ride before it stops and he rolls his ankle and falls awkwardly right in front of his partner. "Oh my goodness! Are you hurt?" asks his boyfriend. "Heck yeah I'm hurt! I went around five times and you didn't wave to me once!"

*   *   *

What's worse than your doctor telling you that you have Aids?

Your father telling you.

*   *   *

Henry: If you woke up in the woods with Vaseline all over your ass, would you tell anyone?
Lester: Hell no!
Henry: Wanna go camping?

*   *   *

Willie proclaims to Dan. "I think my roommate is gay." "What makes you think that?" asked Dan. "He closes his eyes every time I kiss him goodnight."

*   *   *

How do you know for sure your roommate's gay?

His dick tastes like shit.

*   *   *

How do you make a gay guy scream really hard?

After your done with him, wipe your dick on the curtains.

PEDOPHILES
(Here kiddie kiddie)

*   *   *

What's so great about having sex with twenty four year olds?

There's twenty of them.

*   *   *

Knock knock.
Who’s there?
Little boy blue.
Little boy blue who?
Michael Jackson.

*   *   *

Did you here that McDonalds dedicated a hamburger in Michael Jackson's name?

It's a little piece of meat shoved between ten year old buns.

*   *   *

What does Michael Jackson and caviar have in common?

They both come on little crackers.

*　　　*　　　*

How do you know when it's bedtime in Michael Jackson's house?

When the big hand touches the little hand.

*　　　*　　　*

Do you know Michael Jackson's alma-matter?

Bring-em Young.

*　　　*　　　*

Isn't it just odd that Michael Jackson was burnt by Pepsi and Richard Pryer was burnt by Coke?

*　　　*　　　*

Since he's mostly plastic; after Michael Jackson died they melted him down and made Lego pieces out of him.

Now, little kids can play with HIM!

*　　　*　　　*

Do you know how Michael Jackson really died?

He had a heart attack when he heard that young men's pants are half off at Walmart.

*   *   *

What's the worst part about screwing a four year old?

Trying to get the blood out of the clown suit.

*   *   *

What's the best part about screwing a four year old?

Watching him break down on the witness stand.

*   *   *

How do you know your girlfriend is too young?

You have to make airplane noises to get your dick in her mouth.

*   *   *

What's black and blue and hates sex?

The little kid in my basement.

*   *   *

A cop rolls up on a car parked in a secluded spot over looking the town. The windows are steamed up so he shines his flashlight in and sees a man sitting in the front seat reading a magazine and in the back seat there is a girl knitting. The cop makes the guy roll down his window and asks him, "What's going on?" "Nothing." "How old are you?" "Thirty one." Then the cop asked, "How old is she?" The man looked at his watch and said, "In ten minutes she'll be eighteen."

*　　　　　*　　　　　*

A man brings his twelve year old daughter to the pharmacist for some birth control. The pharmacist can't believe how young she is. "She's sexually active?" "Fuck no," the man replies. "She just lays there like her mother."

*　　　　　*　　　　　*

What's the best thing about High School girls?

No matter how old we get, they always stay the same age.

*　　　　　*　　　　　*

A clown and a six year old boy are walking hand in hand going into the woods. The sun is setting. The little boy said, "It's spooky in here. I'm getting scared." The clown goes, "You're scared? I have to walk back by myself!"

*　　　　　*　　　　　*

QUICKIES

*   *   *

What's the opposite of Above me?

Blow me.

*   *   *

What's the difference between a band leader and a gynecologist?

A band leader fucks his singers. A gynecologist sucks his fingers.

*   *   *

What's the last sound you hear before a pubic hair hits the ground?

Pfftt.

*   *   *

What's the difference between light and hard?

I can sleep with a light on.

*   *   *

What's the difference between a cop car and a pin cushion?

On a pin cushion, the pricks are on the outside.

*   *   *

How many hipsters does it take to screw in a light bulb?

It's a cool number you never heard of.

*   *   *

What do you get when you cross a dyslexic, an atheist, and an insomniac?

Someone who stays up all night wondering if there really is a DOG.

*   *   *

How do you recycle a used rubber?

Turn it inside out and shake the fuck out of it.

*   *   *

What do you do with 365 used condoms?

Make a tire out of them and call it a Good Year.

*   *   *

What do you have if you have nuts on your wall?
Wall nuts.

*   *   *

What do you have if you have nuts on your chest?
Chest nuts.

*   *   *

What do you have if you have nuts on your chin?
A dick in your mouth!

*   *   *

Where is the best place for a person with one leg to work?

I-Hop.

*   *   *

What do you call a woman with one tit?

Eileen.

*   *   *

What does Cherrios, Tide, and Woody Allen have in common?

They all come in a yellow box.

*   *   *

What's the difference between ooh and ahh?

About 3 inches.

*   *   *

What's the difference between Herpes and Mono?

You get Mono from snatching a kiss.

*   *   *

A couple of guys are watching the game on T.V. when the town's siren calls the firemen to the station. One guy gets up to leave and his friends ask, "Where are you going? You're not a fireman." He says, "No, but my girlfriend's husband is!"

*   *   *

What's the difference between a hormone and a vitamin?

You can't hear a vitamin.

*   *   *

What's the difference between a whore and a bitch?

A whore fucks everyone.
A bitch fucks everyone but you.

*   *   *

Hear about the stewardess that backed into the propeller?

Disaster.

*   *   *

What do you call a delivery van full of vibrators?

Toys for twats.

*   *   *

What do you call delivery van full of vibrators driven by a lesbian?

Dick van Dyke.

*   *   *

What do you do if a maxi-pad catches fire?

Tampon it.

*   *   *

What's 69+69?

Diner for 4.

*   *   *

What's 68?

You do me and I'll owe you one.

*   *   *

Why is the speed limit of sex 68?

Any faster and you'll blow a rod.

*   *   *

What's 6.9?

A good time interrupted by a period.

*   *   *

What do you call 69 in China?

Tu can chew.

*   *   *

What is the square root of 69?

Ate something.

* * *

What do you call a guy with no arms and no legs sitting on your door step?
Matt.

What do you call a guy with no arms and no legs if you bring him in and hang him on the wall?
Art.

What do you call two guys with no arms and no legs hanging on your wall?
Curt and Rod.

What do you call a guy with no arms and no legs that's buried under a pile of leaves?
Rustle.

What do you call a guy with no arms and no legs when you throw him across the water?
Skip.

What do you call the same guy with no arms and no legs when you leave him in the water?
Bob.

What do you call guy with no arms and legs that's has been on your lawn all night?
Dewey.

What do you call a guy with no arms and no legs going over a fence?
Homer.

What do you call a GIRL with no arms and no legs?
Muffy.

What did the kid with no arms and no legs get for Christmas?
Cancer.

What do you call a kid with no arms no legs and a patch on his eye?
Names.

* * *

Why do Bulimics love KFC?

It comes with a bucket.

* * *

D.A.M.

Mothers against Dyslexia.

* * *

What's green and yellow and eats nuts?

Gonorrhea.

* * *

What's black and eats pussy?

Cervical cancer.

WORK

(The floggings will continue until morale improves.)

* * *

What job is more stressful than yours?
A bank guard in Alaska...
Everyone that comes in is wearing a ski mask.

* * *

A guy going through the express lane at the supermarket places his items on the conveyor belt. A bag of chips, a six pack of beer, a T.V. dinner, and a stick of deodorant. The cute girl checking him out, looks at his items and says, "Single huh?" The guy responds sarcastically, "Gee, how'd you guess?" She says, "Because your ugly."

* * *

A guy goes into a clock repair business, browses the inventory and moseys up to the cute sales girl at the counter. He pulls down his pants, pulls his meat out of his drawers and slaps it on the counter. The salesgirl gazes at his impressive equipment and informs him of the confusion. "Sir. This is a CLOCK shop."
"I know," he said. "I was just wondering if you could put two hands and a face on this."

*　　　　*　　　　*

The Bronx Zoo gets a new female gorilla. She is in heat and is very belligerent towards the guests. She needs sex. The zookeeper asked the custodian if he wouldn't mind having sex with the creature for five hundred dollars. The custodian agreed but said, "I'm going to need a week to come up with five hundred bucks!"

*　　　　*　　　　*

A manager is faced with a decision: One of the two new-hires has to go. It's either Jack, or it's Jill. He passes Jill in the hallway and runs it by her. "I need to lay you or Jack off." She says, "Jack off! I'm on break."

*　　　　*　　　　*

A guy peeks his head into a barber shop and asks the barber, "How long?" The barber counts the customers in front of him and says, "About forty five minutes." The guy leaves. The next day he peeks his head in again, "How long?" The barber says, "About an hour." The guy leaves. This goes on all week and when he comes by on Saturday the place is pretty busy. He still sticks his head in and asks, "How long?" The barber says your going to have to give me about an hour and a half. The guy leaves. The barber tells his friend about this guy doing that all week but never comes back. "Go follow him and see where he goes." His friend takes off after him. He comes back ten minutes later laughing his ass off. The barber asks, "Did you follow that guy?" "Yeah," he says in his break of laughter. "Where does he go?" His friend says, "Your house!"

*   *   *

A man applies for a job at the Post Office. The interviewer asked him, "Are you a veteran?" “Yes, I did two tours over in Afghanistan.” “Well that’s good because that gives you five extra points towards your test score. You wouldn’t happen to be disabled are you?” “As a matter of fact I am. I lost my testicles in a mortar explosion.” “That’s fantastic! That gives you ten more points and secures you a job. You can start Monday at nine o’clock.” The guy says, “Nine? I thought mailmen started at seven.” “Oh, we do. But for the first two hours we just stand around and scratch our balls.”

*   *   *

"I got fired from the pickle factory today," Kevin said. "What did you do?" asked Pat. "I stuck my my dick in the pickle slicer." "Are you okay?" "Yeah," Kevin replied. "What happened to the pickle slicer then?" Kevin said, "They fired her too."

*   *   *

A mailman was retiring after 35 years on the job. As he was walking the route for the last time his customers were greeting him with gifts and well wishes. One family came to the door with a collection of fishing lures. Another guy gave him a box of cigars and another bought him a bottle of scotch. He was having a great day.

When he got to one house he was greeted by a woman wearing a lace negligee. She took him by the hand and led him to the bedroom, took off his uniform and gave him the best sex he's had in years. When they were done she reached over to her night stand and handed him a dollar. "What's this for?" he asked. "This was all my husband's idea. I told him you were retiring and he said, "Fuck him. Give a buck!"

*   *   *

A New York cab driver cruising for fares picks up a distinguished English gentleman who says he wants to go to London. He has a fear of flying and would feel more comfortable in the back of a car. The gent said he would pay handsomely. The cabby had friends that worked at J.F.K. airport so they loaded his cab in the back of a cargo plane, flew to Heathrow airport and then drove into London. He lets his fare out at Piccadilly who then pays him five hundred dollars for the ride plus another hundred as a tip. The best day he's ever had as a cab driver.

He's never been to London before so he decides to take in some sights. As he's driving around he realizes he might as well pick up some fares here too. The first guy who flags him down is a black guy who says he'd pay him five hundred dollars to take him to New York. "Holy Shit!" This is one lucky day. "Where to buddy?" he asks. "123rd and Lexington." The cabby says, "Bitch! I don't go to Harlem!"

*   *   *

A guy sticks his head into a barber shop and asks, "Bob Peters here?"

The barber responded, "No. We just cut hair!"

*   *   *

There I was, sitting at the bar, staring at my drink when a large, trouble-making biker steps up next to me, grabs my drink and gulps it down in one swig. "Well, whatcha gonna do about it?" he asked menacingly. I burst into tears. "Come on, man," the biker says. "I didn't think you'd CRY. I can't stand to see a man crying." "This is the worst day of my life," I say. "I'm a complete failure. I was late to a meeting and my boss fired me. When I went to the parking lot I found my car had been stolen and I don't have any insurance. I left my wallet in the cab I took home. I found my old lady in bed with my neighbor and then my own dog bit me." "So I came to this bar to work up the courage to put an end to it all. I buy a drink, I drop a capsule in it and sit here watching the poison dissolve. Then you, you jack-ass, show up and drink the whole damn thing! But enough about me, how's your day going?"

* * *

A guy works in a diamond mine and the manager is constantly accusing him of stealing diamonds. Everyday he walks out of the mine pushing a wheelbarrow with a sheet over it. The boss would pop out of nowhere, "A-ha!" He'd whip the sheet back expecting to catch him red handed. Nothing. Everyday this would happen.

Week after week until he just got sick of it and quit. The boss was confused. "Why quit? Just because we make a few accusations here and there?" "No," replied the guy. "I just can't work for anyone too stupid to realize I've been stealing their wheelbarrows."

* * *

A guy applies for a job as a piano player in a tavern. The demonstration that he gives the manager just blows him away. The manager said that he's never heard such talent in his whole life. "What was the name of that song anyway?" "It's called, Your father's a bore but your mother's a whore." "Interesting title. You're hired! You can start right now, just keep playing beautiful songs." He plays another incredible melody. "What was that called?" "The smegma on my penis reeks of shit," he says. "That's a gross name for a song, but it's a great melody!" His next song is titled, "Your sister's snatch is on fire, in G minor."

It's a huge hit with the patrons. His playing really starts packing in the customers. After playing half the night, he excuses himself to the crowd for a short break. When he returns from the bathroom the manager runs over to him, "Do you know your fly's undone and your dick's hanging out?" He says, "Know it? I wrote it!"

* * *

What do you call a hooker with a runny nose?

Full.

* * *

A supervisor tells the shop forman about one of his employes that calls in sick every Monday. "Fire him!" the forman demands. The supervisor explains that he doesn't want to do that because Tuesday through Friday he out performs all the other workers. The forman tells the supervisor to get to the bottom of this because he might have a problem. After calling in sick on Monday again, the supervisor calls the guy into his office on Tuesday morning and asks him what's going on. "Do you have a drinking problem?" “No," he replied. "Is it drugs?" "No, it's nothing like that." "Then what's the deal? Every Monday you call me and tell me your sick." "Well," the man reluctantly explains. "It's my sister. She's married to this real prick. Every Sunday night he goes out bowling with his league and comes home drunk and abusive. She comes over to my house upset and I have to console her. One thing leads to another and we end up having sex all night long and Monday morning I'm just too tired to come to work." "With your sister?" The boss yells. "That's disgusting!" The man said, "Hey, I told you I was sick!"

*   *   *

A guy shows up at work an hour late with a black eye, busted lip and his arm in a sling. He told his boss that he fell down a flight of stairs. His boss replied,
"And that took you an hour?"

SPORTS
(Ball Play)

*   *   *

Quick. Name three N.F.L. teams whose name begins with the letter F.

The Falcons, The Forty Niners and The Fucking Cowboys.

*   *   *

What's the hardest part about being a Dallas Cowboy fan?

Having to tell your parents you're gay.

*   *   *

How do you get an Oakland Raider fan off your porch?

Pay him for the pizza.

*　　　　*　　　　*

A few N.Y. Giant fans at a home game complained to security about an Eagle's fan lying down, taking up 4 seats in the front row, cursing. The guard goes down there and the Eagle's fan won't move and is babbling swear words. It took security a while to get an answer when they asked, "Where did you come from?" He finally pointed skyward and mumbled, "The upper level."

*　　　　*　　　　*

Steve's friends were marveling over his new glow-in-the-dark golf ball that's impossible to lose. He explained to them, "If you hit it in tall grass, a flag will pop out of it and a whistle will sound. If you hit it in the water hazard, it floats and it has a fan to blow it back to land." His friends agree that it is the best invention ever. "Where did you get it?" Steve replied proudly, "I found it!"

*　　　　*　　　　*

What's the difference between a tribe of pygmies and a girls track team?

One is a cunning bunch of runts.

*　　　　*　　　　*

"Fore!" Jason looks too late to see what's coming. Bam! He gets nailed with a golf ball. Doubled over in pain, cupping his hands to his crotch, the pretty young lady that hit it offers her help. She unzips his pants and rubs his penis and balls. After a minute she asks, "There, does that feel better?" "Yeah, but my thumb still hurts like hell!"

*   *   *

A guy is at his first Superbowl. During the game he keeps eyeing with his binoculars, an open seat right on the fifty yard line just a few rows up from the players. At half time he sneaks down from his nosebleed seat and asked the man sitting there if the seat was taken. The man says, "No," and offers it to him. "My God! These are great seats. Who does this one belong to?" "Oh, my wife. She died so the seat is yours now." "You didn't have anyone else that wanted to come? No family or friends?"
"Nah," the man replied. "They're all at her funeral."

*   *   *

Why do basketball players make horrible porn actors?

Because they always dribble before they shoot.

*   *   *

Peekaboo Street, the gold medal winning alpine skier, was hospitalized after careening off coarse at the Super G in Switzerland. Her recovery from broken legs and torn ligaments was long and arduous. To show her gratitude to the hospital staff that treated her so well, she donated money to add a wing to the medical center.
It's called 'The Peekaboo I.C.U.'

*   *   *

Do you know the definition of endless love?

Stevie Wonder and Ray Charles playing tennis.

*   *   *

A golfer and his wife are playing a round and the man hooks his drive into the woods. When he finds his ball he is perplexed on how to get it back on the fairway. He's almost surrounded by trees. His wife suggest he lean on shot and put it right through the open maintenance barn doors because the fairway is right on the other side. The golfer tries her recommendation but hits the top of the barn door and the ball comes back and hits his wife in the head and kills her.

A week later the same golfer is out there with his friend and hooks from the same tee right to the same spot. The friend makes the suggestion that he lean on the ball and knock it through the open barn doors because the fairway is right on the other side. The guy says, "Fuck that! The last time I tried that, I drew a seven."

*   *   *

Why do they call it golf?

All the other four letter words were taken.

*   *   *

Little Johnny's parents are getting divorced. The judge offers him the rare opportunity to decide which parent he wants to live with. "Would you like to live with your Dad?" "No way! He beats me," Johnny said. "So, you want to live with your Mommy then?" Johnny says, "Hell no! She beats me too." "Then who do you want to live with?" asked the judge. "I want to live with the Chicago Cubs." Johnny replied. "The Cubs? Why the Cubs?" "Because," said Johnny, "They don't beat anyone!"

Christianity

(A damn good book)

*   *   *

What goes clippity clop, clippity clop, clippity clop, BANG, BANG, clippity clop, clippity clop?

An Amish drive by.

*   *   *

A guy in a trench coat runs up and flashes the three nuns on a bench.
Two had a stroke. The third wouldn't even touch it.

*   *   *

A man arrives at the pearly gates and Saint Peter is not expecting him. "I'm sorry sir. Are you sure you are supposed to be up here?" "Of course! I certainly don't belong down there," said the man. Saint Peter goes through his book again and even cross referenced his social security number but there's no record of him. "I'm sorry sir. There seems to be a mix up. Have you done any good deeds in your life?" "Of course I have!" the man said angrily. "How about that time that I got that old lady's purse back from the biker gang that stole it? Then I ran over all their bikes with my car so they couldn't harm anyone else." Saint Peter is frantically flipping through his book. "I'm sorry sir. I don't have any record of such a heroic deed. When did that happen?"
The guy said, "About a minute ago."

*   *   *

A woman dies while having a simple operation. When she arrives in heaven she was told that there was a mixup and she has plenty of life to live. When she awoke in the hospital, she decides to stay there a while and have some work done. She figured, if she has the time, she is going to make the most of it.

She gets a facelift, a tummy tuck, a boob job, a butt lift, lyposuction and some Botox. She was in the hospital a few weeks. When she finally walked out, she got hit by a bus and was killed. She arrived up in heaven and asked God, "Why did you do this to me? You said I had plenty of time." God said, "My bad! I didn't recognize you."

*   *   *

Quasimoto, the hunchback of Notre Dame, has had enough of the bell ringing and suddenly quits. The Arch Bishop is desperate for a replacement before Sundays mass. He puts an ad in the paper and gets a lot of applicants. None of which have the strength or the rhythm to ring the bell in the tower. After interviewing over two hundred people he thinks he has found his man. Although an unlikely job recipient due to him not having arms, this guy is sufficient.

He rings the bell by getting a running start and smashing into the bell with his head. He can even ring the two hundred pound bell twelve times. While ringing the bell for Sundays mass he loses his timing and misses the bell causing him to fall to his death. The crowd gathered around and a policeman asked if anyone knew this man. The Arch Bishop said, "I don't know his name, but his face rings a bell."

*   *   *

The Arch Bishop needs another bell ringer for the afternoon mass. He goes through the crowd asking if anyone would like the job. One man steps forward but he too is missing both his arms. The Arch Bishop gives him a chance. He climbs the bell tower steps, gets a running start and smashes the bell with his face. BONG! He steps back to do it again but misses the swinging bell and falls to his death. The crowd gathers around again and the cop pushes his way through and asked if anyone knows THIS man. The Arch Bishop again speaks up, "I don't know his name either but he's a dead ringer for his brother."

*   *   *

A man in his late sixties goes into a confession booth at church. The priest asks him what his sin was. "Father, I've been married to the same woman for forty six years and have never once committed adultery until last night. While at the bar, I struck up a conversation with two very beautiful young ladies. We got along famously. We talked for hours. We even started dancing together. The bar closed and we went back to their apartment and carried on drinking and dancing. Well, one thing led to another and long story short, we ended up having sex all night long and well into the morning." "How long has it been since your last confession?" the priest asked. "Father, I've never been to confession before. I'm not even Catholic!" "Then why are you telling me this?" The guy said, "Are you kidding me? I'm telling everybody!"

* * *

Four people die and go up to the pearly gates to be greeted by Saint Peter. Three men and one woman. Saint Peter asked them how they all died at relatively the same time. They all responded at once. Yelling and trying to talk over one another. Saint Peter brought them to order saying, "Ladies first." The woman proclaimed, "This is my husband and he came home early from work ranting and raving about me cheating on him. He went into the bathroom, then the bedroom and came out with a gun and shot me! That's all I know." Saint Peter asked her husband if this is true. "Hell yeah! I know this bitch is cheating on me! I found the toilet seat up, the bed spread was on the floor and this asshole was hanging out of my bedroom window. So I killed him, shot her and turned the gun on myself."

Saint Peter asked the other man if he was really having an affair with his wife. "Fuck no! I'm not fucking that fat bitch! I'm the maintenance man in their apartment building and I fell from the the fifth floor window but I caught myself on their window sill right below. I was worried I was going to be there for hours but he opened the window right away. I thought I was saved! But noooo! This schmuck bashes my knuckles with a hammer so I fell four stories. I landed in some big bushes and I thought I was saved again and was thanking God my life was spared. Then this dickhead throws a refrigerator down on top of me! That's all I know. Saint Peter bows his head in sorrow at this tragedy that has just unfolded. To the last man he asked, "How did you reach your demise?" He says with a shrug, "I don't even know. I'm sitting in this refrigerator, minding my own business..."

*   *   *

Two nuns are riding their bicycles through town back to the Abby. They decide to take a shortcut through some cobblestone streets. One nun says, "I've never come this way before." The other replies, "Yeah! It's the cobbles."

*   *   *

Paddy is a good catholic. He goes to confession and tells the priest that he used the Lord's name in vain while playing golf this morning. The priest says, "I understand, I play a little golf myself you know." Paddy says, "I hit a beautiful, three hundred yard drive but the wind caught it and blew it in the rough." "Is that when you used the Lord's name in vain?" "No father. I used my new wood to get out of the tall grass and it rolled off the green right into the sand trap." "I bet THAT'S when you said it. Huh?" "No father. I chipped it back on to the green and got the ball six inches from the hole." The priest shouted, "Don't tell me you missed that God damn putt!"

*   *   *

What's the difference between a nun and a woman taking a bath?

The nun has hope in her soul.

*   *   *

The Pope has fallen ill and the Vatican doctor, after numerous tests, finds that the Pope has Testiculitis. He informs the Cardinals and Arch Bishop that the Pope's balls are full and he needs immediate release. "The Pope is not allowed to have sex!" they respond. The doctor insists that if he doesn't get his balls drained he's going to die. They discuss the issue at length and decide that the Pope should be excused from the rules just this one time for the good of the church. They talk this over with the Pope. After some convincing, the Pope agrees to have his first woman, but only under three conditions... "First, the woman must be blind so she can't see with whom she's having sex. Second, the woman must be deaf so she can't figure out she's in the Vatican." They all agree. "What's the third condition?" they ask. The Pope whispers his answer..."Big tits!"

* * *

What does a priest and a pimple have in common?

They both come on a boy's face when he turns thirteen.

* * *

Why cant Jesus eat M&Ms?

They fall through the holes in his hands.

* * *

Little Johnny came home from Catholic school with two black eyes. His parents asked him what happened. He explained, "Well, my fat ass teacher was sitting in front of me when we were singing the hymns. When she stood up, she had a wedgie. I pulled her dress out of her crack and she smacked me!" His dad asked, "She gave you two black eyes from one smack?" "No," Johnny said. "When she turned back around, I tried to be nice and I tucked it back in."

*　　　　*　　　　*

Three nuns where asked by mother superior to help tidy up the convent and paint a few rooms. As they where painting the first room they realized that they'd better take off their habits so they wouldn't get paint on them. They were painting away, stark naked, flicking paint on each other and giggling like silly school girls. Suddenly, they heard a knock on the door. One nun asked, "Who is it?" "I'm the blind man. Mother superior asked me to come talk to you." As she reached for the door knob to let him in the other nuns shrieked. "What are you doing? You can't just let him in! He’s a man and we don't have our clothes on!” "Yeah, but he's a BLIND man. He won't know we're naked if we don't tell him!" said the first nun. After some thought and discussion, "Oh, okay let him in," they said in agreement. She opened the door, the man walks in and says, "Nice tits sister! Where do you want me to hang the blinds?"

*　　　　*　　　　*

Three priests take the boat out for a day of fishing and bring along a couple of alter boys. They hit rough seas and the boat starts sinking. One priest says, "Save the boys!" Another says, "Fuck the boys!" The third asked, "Do we have time?"

*　　　　*　　　　*

A priest is passing the freshly baptized baby back to the proud papa. The priest says, "That's a hansom lad you have there." The father says, "It's a girl. You're holding my thumb."

*   *   *

An old priest is retiring. He gives the replacement priest a tour of the church and introduces him to the staff. He leaves him a list of responsibilities and the list of repentance in the confessional. The first confession the new priest hears is from a young woman who says she had given oral sex to her prom date. The priest checks the list for the repentance and there is nothing on the list about that. The young priest looks under oral sex, fellatio and blow jobs. Nothing. Panicked, he looks out of the confession booth for help. He sees an alter boy walking past. "Psst! Hey kid. "What did the old priest give for a blow job?" The alter boy responded, "Usually some candy and a Coke."

*   *   *

Three couples are in the pastors office being interviewed because they all want to become part of the church. There's a newlywed couple, a middle age couple and an elderly couple. The pastor speaks with them all and sends them away with the request that they practice sexual abstinence for thirty days. When they return a month later the pastor asks the elderly couple if they abstained. The elderly couple told him that they haven't had sex in years. "Well, not much of a sacrifice, but welcome to our church." He asked the middle age couple if they abstained. "The last few days were difficult but we really want to become part of your congregation, so yes, we abstained." "Good," said the pastor. "Welcome to our church." He turned to the newlyweds, who now have their heads hanging in shame. "Were you able to abstain?" "No sir," was their meek reply. "How long did you last then?" "Only three days sir." "Three days? What happened?" "Well," the young man began. "We're fixing up our new place together and she bent over to pick up some paint and the urge took over and I had to have her right then and there." The pastor was very disappointed and told them that they're no longer welcome in the church. "That's cool," said the young man. "We're no longer allowed in Home Depot either."

JEWISH
(Oy Vey!)

A priest and a rabbi were walking through the park and they see a nine year old boy. The priest asked, “You wanna screw him?” The rabbi says, “Out of what?”

* * *

What's brown and hides in the attic?

The Diarrhea of Ann Frank.

* * *

Hear about the new German microwave?

It seats forty.

* * *

What’s the difference between a Jew and a pizza?

A pizza doesn’t scream in the oven.

*   *   *

How do wash your Genitals?

Same as you wash your Jew.

*   *   *

As my wife and I were driving through a rural town in Ohio we saw a theatre sign advertising; Tonight only...'MELVIN THE MAGNIFICENT JEW.' Curiosity got the best of us. The place was packed. The lights finally dimmed and out walked an elderly man in a robe. When the spotlight came upon him he removed his robe and stood before us wearing nothing but a yamaka. He had the largest penis anyone had ever seen. HUGE! He walked over to a table lined with walnuts. He picked up his manhood with both hands and smashed all the nuts to bits. The place erupted in a standing ovation that lasted well after Melvin left the stage.

Twenty years later we were driving through that town again and we saw the same sign.
Tonight only...'MELVIN THE MAGNIFICENT JEW.' We couldn't believe it. The place was packed again. When Melvin walked out and removed his robe. We couldn't believe he looked exactly the same. He hadn't changed a bit. He walked over to a table lined with coconuts. He picked up his tremendous manhood with both hands and smashed all the coconuts, raining milk on the audience like a Gallagher show. A ten minute standing ovation ensued.

After the show we went backstage to meet Melvin. "Twenty years ago you smashed walnuts. Why did you switch to coconuts?" Melvin told us, "Eh. My eyesight ain't what it used to be."

*   *   *

How many Jews can you fit in a Volkswagen?

Two in the front, two in the back and five hundred in the ashtray.

*   *   *

Did you hear about the Japanese-Jewish restaurant?

It's called Sosueme.

*   *   *

What do you call a gay Jew?

A Heblew.

*   *   *

Why do Jews have big noses?

Because the air is free.

*   *   *

A guy sees a another man at the end of the bar that looks just like Hitler. He goes up and asks him if he really was Hitler. He jumps up and screams, "For crying out loud! YES! I'm Adolf Hitler okay? I killed six million Jews and a Canadian. The guy says, "Wait! Why did you kill a Canadian?" Hitler goes, "See what I mean? Nobody cares about the Jews!"

*   *   *

How do you drive a Jew crazy?

Put him in a round room and tell him there's a penny in the corner.

*   *   *

What's the great Jewish dilemma?

Free bacon.

*   *   *

How was copper wire invented?

Two jews fighting over a penny.

*   *   *

What's the difference between a Jew and a canoe?

A canoe tips.

*   *   *

What's the difference between the Boy Scouts and the Jews?

The Boy Scouts come home from camp.

*   *   *

An old Jewish vagabond goes into a whorehouse and asked to see Katarina. The madam says Katarina is unavailable but if he'd like to choose from some of the other girls, they might be more within his price range. "No, I'll wait," says the man. "Sir, Katarina is one thousand dollars for the hour. These girls might be more suitable for you." The man pulls out a wad of cash and counts out ten, hundred dollar bills. The Madam calls Katarina down and she takes him upstairs. An hour later he happily leaves.

He comes back the next night still wearing the same clothes and asked for Katarina. The madam insists that she is still a thousand dollars. "That's okay." He then peels off ten one hundreds. Katarina takes him upstairs and then an hour later he leaves happy. He returns again the next night still wearing those beat up old clothes and makes the same request. As Katarina is helping him put on his dirty old trench coat upon completion of the deed, she says to the man, “I've never had a customer come back two nights in a row no less three. You're very intriguing to me. Where are you from?" "Minsk," the man replies. "Minsk? Russia?" Katarina reaffirms. "My sister lives in Minsk." "Yeah, Nichola," the man says. "You know my sister?"
"Sure," the man says. "She gave me three grand to give to you."

*   *   *

Katy was pissing and moaning to Joseph about all the wrongs that the Jewish people have done to this world. "They are trying to rule the world through economics. They sunk the Titanic. They killed baby Jesus and they're trying promote their anti-Christian ways through the media!" Joseph interrupted her rant. "Wait! What? The Jews sunk the Titanic? I thought it was an iceberg." Katy said, "Iceberg, Steinberg, Goldberg. They're all the same!”

*   *   *

An old Jewish man tells his Rabbi that he had won three million dollars in the lottery. The Rabbi shouts, “That’s wonderful! What are you going to do with all that money?” “Well, I’m old. I’m going to give one million to my kids so their families can play. I’ll give another million to charity, and the last million I’m giving to the church. “Fantastic!” yells the Rabbi. The guy continues, “On one condition. You have to erect a life sized statue of Hitler out front.” “What? A statue of Hitler in front of a synagog? Why?” asked the Rabbi. “Because he’s the one that tattooed the winning numbers on my arm.”

*   *   *

A Jewish woman says to the Pollock in bed, "I thought you Poles were thick."
He said, "I thought you Jews were tight!"

*   *   *

A Jewish guy is on his knees praying to God every night. "Please God, let me win the lottery." The drawing comes around and nothing. The next night; "Please God, I need this. Let me win the lottery." Saturday’s drawing; nope. "Please, oh please, let me win the lottery! I promise I'll do good things with the money." The drawing comes around and he doesn't win again. "Please God. Let me please win the lottery. I promise I'll be forever in your dept." All of a sudden there's a load clap of thunder in the sky. The clouds slowly part and a beam of light shines from the heavens. God’s booming voice overwhelms him. "Sal! You cheap bastard! Buy a damn ticket!"

*   *   *

A Jewish guy moves his elderly father to the Jewish nursing home. A week after he's admitted, his son comes back to visit. "So, Dad, how do you like it here?" "I hate it! I want to leave!" was Dad's response. "But Dad, this is where you always wanted to spend your golden years. The synagog is right next door. There's a lake view and everything. What's not to like?" "This place is filled with a bunch of miserable old Jews. They're always pissing and moaning about everything. It's just depressing. I want to leave!" "But Dad," contests his son, "Where do you want to go?" "There's an Irish nursing home down the street. I want to go there." "C'mon Dad! An Irish nursing home? Really? Why would you want to go there?" "Because I can hear them laughing all the time. It sounds like they're always having fun. Please take me there!" They gather all of his belongings, discharge out of the Jewish nursing home and he admits him into the Irish nursing home.

The son returns the following weekend to visit, thinking he would just be bringing him back to Jewish nursing home. "So Dad, how do you like it here?" "I love it here! This place is great!" was Dads surprising response. "What? Really? What's so great about this place?" Dad's face lights up as he begins to explain. "The Irish are always in a good mood and they joke around all the time. It's just fun! They even have nicknames for each other." "Nicknames? Like what?" inquires his son. Dad continues excitedly, "Do you see that bald guy? They call him Curly. He doesn't have a stitch of hair on his head." "That's pretty funny Dad, what else?" "See that guy in the wheelchair? They call him Speedy. Speedy Gonzales! He doesn't even have legs." "That great Dad," the son says sarcastically. "How about you? Do you have a nickname yet?" "Yeah, as a matter of fact I do." "Really? You've only been here a week. What's your nickname?" "Well, you know that I haven't had sex in twenty years since your mom died?
They call me 'The Fuckin' Jew!"

ARABS
(Does THIS mean war?)

I'd fly six thousand miles to smoke a camel.

*   *   *

Did you hear about the new Iraqi flag?

It's a white star on a white background.

*   *   *

Did you hear about the Arab terrorist that tried to blow up our Presidents limousine?

He burnt his lips on the tailpipe.

*   *   *

What should Iraq do with its Air Defense System?

Get a refund.

*   *   *

Why aren't there any Walmarts in Afghanistan?

Because there's a Target around every corner

*   *   *

What's the definition of a damn shame?

A bus full of Arabs going off a cliff with two empty seats.

*   *   *

What's the difference between American pilots and Arab pilots?

American pilots break ground and fly into the wind.

*   *   *

If an Iraqi and an Iranian both jump off the top of a tall building in a race to martyrdom, who wins?

Society.

*   *   *

Why do Arabs smell bad?

So blind people can hate them too.

*   *   *

Bin Laden cocktail:

Two shots and a splash of water.

*   *   *

Bin Laden's fate was Sealed.

*   *   *

Now he has seventy two Sturgeon.

*   *   *

How come the Taliban never go out drinking?

They can stay home and get bombed.

*   *   *

What's the difference between a Ferrari and a stack of dead Muslims.

I don't have a Ferrari in my garage.

*   *   *

Two Arabs were riding their camel across the desert and the camel collapsed from exhaustion. They dragged the animal over to an oasis but he wouldn't drink. One said, "We'll make him drink. I'll hold his head to the water and you suck on his ass." After a few minutes of this, the Arab in the back called out, "Pick his head up a little. I'm just getting mud!"

*   *   *

Two families move from Afghanistan to America. Upon arrival the two fathers make a bet: In a years time, whichever family had become more Americanized would win.

A year later they met. The first Afghan said, “My son is playing baseball, I had McDonald’s for breakfast and I’m on way to shoot some pool and drink some Bud. How about you? The second man replied, “Fuck you, Rag head!”

SUDANESE
(Formally Ethiopian)

*   *   *

Ever had Sudanese food?

Neither have they.

*   *   *

What do you call a Sudanese with buck teeth?

A rake.

*   *   *

What do you call a Sudanese with a yeast infection?

A Quarter pounder with cheese.

*   *   *

What do you call a Sudanese with big feet?

A golf club.

*   *   *

What do you call a Sudanese with a hair net?

A Lacrosse stick.

*   *   *

What's black and covered with cobwebs?

A Sudanese asshole.

*   *   *

What do you call a Sudanese with a dime on his head?

A nail.

*   *   *

What's the meanest thing you call give a Sudanese person?

An after dinner mint.

*   *   *

What’s another name for a Sudanese family portrait?

Barcode.

*   *   *

What’s the positive thing about being Sudanese?

The H.I.V.

*   *   *

Why do Sudanese fathers masturbate 3 times a day?

Gotta feed the babies!

*   *   *

What is 6-12-6?

The measurements of Miss Sudan.

*   *   *

But I'm in the market for a mid size Sudan.

INDIANS
(Taxi and Casino)

*　　　　*　　　　*

What color was the ground at General Custers last stand?

White. Them Injuns just kept coming and coming.

*　　　　*　　　　*

Who killed more Indians than General Custer?

Union Carbide.

*　　　　*　　　　*

The Fugowi tribe is a small group of nomads.
They wander around lost saying, "Where the Fugowi?
Where the Fugowi?"

*　　　　*　　　　*

The Lone Ranger and Tonto were traveling through a canyon when they encountered fifty Indian warriors up ahead. They turned around and there were a hundred more coming from the rear. They looked up, and on either side of the canyon walls were hordes of pissed off Indians. The Lone Ranger said to Tonto, "Well old friend, I guess there's not much we can do." Tonto said, "What do you mean WE; white boy?"

*   *   *

Keith was trekking through Arizona and came across an Indian lying on his blanket with a boner pointing skyward. "Whatcha doing?" Keith asked. "Me telling time." "Really? What time is it?" The Indian says, Twelve thirty." Keith looked at his watch, "Your right!" he said impressed. He walks on. He soon comes across another Indian with a hard-on. "Whatcha doing?" "Me telling time." "What time you got?" The Indian says, "One twenty." Keith checked his watch again and he too was correct. "Huh!" Later he comes across another Indian lying on his blanket masturbating. Curious, Keith asked, "Whatcha doing? Tellin time?" The Indian says, "Not yet. Me winding watch."

*   *   *

Why do Indians have that red dot on their head?

When they turn eighteen, they scratch it off to see if they won a taxi, a motel or a convenience store.

*   *   *

Haji has been in the United States on a student visa for months. He becomes very ill. He goes to doctor after doctor trying to cure his illness. Finally he finds an Indian doctor that said he can help. "Take this bucket into the next room and take a dump in it. Then piss in it. Shake it around, stick your head in there and take a few deep whiffs."

Haji comes out of the other room afterwards and tells the doctor that he feels much better now. The doctor says, "Yeah, you were just homesick."

CHINESE

(-.-)

* * *

The problem with Chinese chicks:

A half hour later your horny again.

* * *

A Chinese guy was pissing in a urinal when a black guy rushed through the door and started pissing next to him. "Phew! I just made it!" he says with relief. The Chinese guy takes a look at his dong and says, "Can you make one for me?"

* * *

Bobby goes to Hong Kong on business and visited a few brothels and a rub and tug parlor called Massage Myrod. After he came home he noticed some discoloration on his little penis and some brothel sprouts appeared on his balls. After a few visits to different doctors, they all gave him the same prognosis. "You have Hong Kong Dong. It must be removed or you could die." Bobby is distraught to say the least. In an act of desperation he goes back to Hong Kong to talk to a Chinese doctor. "The doctors in America tell me that it needs to be removed." The Chinese doctor looks at his purple, green and yellow willy and tells him not to worry about having any dramatic surgery. Bobby breathes a sigh of relief. "You can make it better then?" The doctor says, "No. It'll fall off by itself."

*   *   *

What do you call a fat Chinaman?

A Chunk.

*   *   *

A guy goes to his doctor repeatedly about his ongoing headaches. The doctor examines him and runs multiple tests but can't find the problem. He goes from doctor to doctor until one suggests he have his very large penis reduced in length by half. He said the blood loss from his brain during erections is the cause. The guy agonizes over what to do but can't stand the headaches any longer and decides to go through with the procedure.

Now that it's done he feels like less of a man and his headaches have returned as soon as he went back to his normal routine. After a long debate with himself he decides he's going to take his own life. He takes care of all the funeral arrangements and writes his last will and testament. Now all he needs to do is buy a suit for his funeral. He goes to the taylor to pick out a fine suit with the best material he can afford. The Chinese taylor measures him up and down and takes a guess at his inseam because the man doesn't want to be touched down there. "You look like 34 inseam." "No I'm a 36," corrects the man. The taylor apologizes but stands his ground. "No, you look like 34. I can tell." "No," insists the man, 36." The Chinese guy says he's been doing this for forty years and he can tell by looking at him that he's a 34. The man says, "Look, I've been wearing suits for 20 years and I always get a 36 inseam!" The taylor says, "I bet you get some wicked headaches!"

*   *   *

The Chinese restaurant business was slow so the owners put their daughter on the street to make some money. Her first trick asked her for a 69. She said,
"You want a Kung Po pork?"

*   *   *

What's yellow and says, "Cheap, cheap?"

A Chinese prostitute.

JAPANESE

(So Wong Earthquakes)

*   *   *

I had to break up with my girlfriend from Japan.

She was crushed.

*   *   *

It's a shame too. Because now I hear she's radiant.

*   *   *

How many Japanese does it take to change a light bulb?

No need to. They all glow in the dark.

*   *   *

You thought the Japanese were good at math now...

Wait till they all have two heads.

*   *   *

Leave it to the Japanese.

They found a way to X-ray the whole population at once.

*   *   *

Charles is an avid skier who is on a quest to ski every major mountain. He climbed to the top of Mt. Fuji and skied down. Proud of his accomplishment, he decided to send home a postcard from Mt. Fuji with a picture of the mountain on the front. He also picked up a postcard of a scantily clad Geisha for his old college buddy. Unfortunately he mixed up the cards and sent the scenic picture to his friend. His wife got the Geisha card with the message on the back, "Here's the slope that I went down on Sunday."

ESKIMOS

(Frigid bitches)

*　　　　*　　　　*

What do you call a lesbian Eskimo?

A Klondyke.

*　　　　*　　　　*

Why do Eskimos wash their clothes in Tide?

Because it's too freaking cold OUT Tide.

*　　　　*　　　　*

Did you hear about the Eskimo girl that spent the night at her boyfriends?

When she came out she was already three months pregnant.

*　　　　*　　　　*

An Eskimo is stranded on the side of the road with a broken snowmobile. A guy pulls over to lend a hand. He says, "Looks like you blew a seal." The Eskimo quickly wiped his mouth and proclaimed, "No, no! It's just frost!"

GREEKS
(Grease)

*   *   *

Why did the Greek boy run away from home?

He didn't like the way he was being reared.

*   *   *

A Greek and an Italian were arguing over whose cultures were more superior. The Greek began, "We have the Parthenon." The Italian countered, "We have the Coliseum." The Greek continues, "We gave birth to advanced mathematics." "We built the Roman Empire," said the Italian. They go back and forth until the Greek thinks he can end it with this. "We Greeks invented sex!" The Italian replied, "True, but we introduced it women!"

GERMANS
(Sour Krauts)

*   *   *

What do the Germans call their tampons?

Twatstickers.

*   *   *

What's green and flies over Germany?

Snotzies.

*   *   *

What do German men call their penises?

Mine shaft.

*   *   *

Little Heinz pushed his brother off the cliff.

"Look Ma. No Hans!"

*   *   *

An East German wakes up one morning in a good mood for no particular reason. He looks out the window and says, "Good morning sun!" The sun replied, "Good morning Dietrich." Later on, he looks out the window, straight up to the sun and says, "Good afternoon sun!" "Good afternoon Dietrich," said the sun. Just before dinner he goes to the window again and yells out, "Good evening sun!" There was no reply. He repeated, "Good evening sun!" Still no response. He yelled it again on top of his lungs. Finally he heard the sun say, "Kiss my ass Dietrich! I'm in the west now!"

THE IRISH
(McDrunks)

*　　　　*　　　　*

An Irish guy walked OUT of a bar......

*　　　　*　　　　*

Did you hear about the two Irish queers?

Patrick Fitzgerald and Gerald Fitzpatrick.

*　　　　*　　　　*

Kelly was out plowing his field in Ireland. After overturning a rock, a leprechaun climbed out of the hole and started running towards the woods. Kelly jumped down and chased after him. He caught him just before he made it to the trees. "Let me go! Let me go!" shouted the leprechaun. "Not until you grant me my three wishes," The farmer replied. "Okay, just put me down!" Kelly put him down and demanded something he always wanted. "I want a never ending bottle of beer. Make it a Guinness!" "Fine," said the leprechaun. He reached into his little green vest and pulled out a bottle of Guinness. The Irishman opened it and took a big gulp. It filled right back up. Kelly took another big swig and it filled right back up. The farmer drank the whole bottle and it filled right back to the top. "Alright, alright. You have two more wishes. What else do you want?" Kelly thought for a moment. Held up the bottle and said, "Give me two more of these!"

*　　　　*　　　　*

What's green, three miles long and smells like piss?

The St. Patty's day parade.

*　　　　*　　　　*

What’s green and never leaves your back yard?

Patty O'Furniture.

*　　　　*　　　　*

How many Irish guys does it take to screw in a light bulb?

Two. One to hold the bulb and one to drink until the room spins.

*　　　　*　　　　*

What's the difference between an Irish wedding and an Irish wake?

One less drunk.

*　　　　*　　　　*

An Irish gentleman and his wife are sitting in a pub. He whispers, "I love you."
She asks, "Is that YOU talking, or the beer?" He replies, "It's me talking to the beer."

* * *

A guy is getting really drunk in the bar and having no luck with the ladies. A midget walking through the crowd, dressed head to toe in green, catches his eye. He follows the midget to the bathroom. Slurring badly, he asked, "What are you supposed to be, a leprechaun?" "Yes, I am! Since you guessed it, you get three wishes. What do you really, really want?" The drunk is stunned. "I guess all I've ever wanted is money." "Fine," says the leprechaun. "The trunk of your car is filled with more money than you will be able to spend in your life." The drunk starts to run out to his car. "Where are you going? You still have two more wishes." The guy is really excited now. "I also want a really big house." "Okay, you now own the mansion over looking the lake on the other side of town." "Oh my God! Okay. I also want a beautiful woman." "Fine," says the leprechaun. "It is done. You have a Playboy centerfold waiting for you to get home to fool around in your new house." The drunk can hardly contain himself. He starts running out of the bathroom. "Where are you going?" asked the leprechaun. "I'm going to screw my woman in my new house on top of a pile of money." The leprechaun asks, "Aren't going to say thank you? I just gave you everything you've always wanted! You're not even going to ask me if I would like something in return?" "Err, sorry about that. You're right. Is there anything I can do for you?" "Yes," says the leprechaun. "I would very much like a blow job." "What? Fuck that! I don't do that!" said the drunk. The leprechaun says, "Wait a minute. I just gave you everything you always wanted and all I ask in return is a little head. I don't understand." He starts weeping. The drunk feels terrible. "Okay. Don't cry. I'll do it." They go into a stall and the drunk gets the job done. He wipes his mouth and starts to leave. "One more thing," says the leprechaun. "How old are you?" "I'm forty two. Why?" The little fellow asked, "You still believe in leprechauns?"

*   *   *

An Irish guy watches his wife struggle through the door with two cases of beer and a bag of potatoes under each arm. He asked, "Are we having a party?" She said, "No. Why?" He said, "That's a lot of potatoes!"

*   *   *

A guy is traveling through Ireland and stops at a petrol station. "Fill ‘er up please," he said to the attendant. "Sorry mate, we're out of petrol." "Well, could you check the oil for me?" "We're out of oil as well." "Could you just top off the radiator then?"

"No. We don't have any water here." "What kind of petrol station is this?" "Actually," the attendant whispers, "We're just a front for the I.R.A." So the traveler asks,

"Could you just blow up my tires?"

*   *   *

An old Irish toast:

Here’s to our wives and girlfriends;
May they never meet.

*   *   *

Paddy goes into the pub and shouts to the barman, ”Drinks for the house and pour one for yourself!” The bartender complies. “That’ll be fifty pounds.” Paddy says, “I don’t have any money.” The barman throws him out. Paddy comes back ten minutes later. “Drinks for the house!” The barman asks sarcastically, “What? No drink for me?” Paddy says, “No! Your an asshole when you drink!”

ITALIANS
(Goombahs)

*　　　*　　　*

What's the difference between an Italian grandmother and an elephant?

50 pounds and a black dress.

*　　　*　　　*

How does an Italian woman keep her long black hair under control?

She wears long sleeves.

*　　　*　　　*

How can you tell an Italian airplane?

It has hair under the wings.

*　　　*　　　*

Why does the new Italian Navy have glass bottom ships?

So they can see the old Italian Navy.

*　　　*　　　*

For sale:
An Italian World War II rifle.

Never fired, only been dropped once.

*　　　*　　　*

How do you know it's an Italian helicopter?

Da big blades; dago guinea, guinea, guinea.
Da little blades; dago wop, wop, wop.

*　　　*　　　*

Why did the Italian soldiers wear brown uniforms?

So nobody would notice that they shit their pants.

*　　　*　　　*

How can you tell if a woman is half Italian and half Irish?

She mashes potatoes with her feet.

*　　　*　　　*

Italian college:

Whats a Matta U.

*   *   *

A stoner sees an Italian barbecuing a chicken on his front porch and tells him, "I don't want to be the bearer of bad news man, but your music quit and your monkey's on fire."

*   *   *

Two Italians were riding the bus and the little old lady behind them got disgusted with their filthy mouths. "Giuseppe, just follow along," Vito said. "Emma come first. Then I come. Thena there are two asses, thena I come again. Thena two more asses thena I come again. Then you takea you two pees, thena I get to come last. Okay?" The lady has had enough. "You foreigners ought to mind your language in public places! You should be ashamed of yourselves!" "But lady," Vito explains. "I was just teaching my friend how to spella Mississippi."

*   *   *

Why is Italy shaped like a boot?

You can't fit all that shit in a sneaker.

*   *   *

Antony the organ grinder is working the crowd in New York city with his pet monkey. The monkey comes up with the cup and Jimmy puts a dollar in it. Kevin asks, "Why did you give him money? You hate Italians!" Jimmy replies, "Yeah, but they're so cute when they're little."

DUH POLISH

*   *   *

A Polish guy comes out of the outhouse and asks his friend for a dollar. His friend curiously gives him a dollar and the Pole throws it into the crap hole and he starts rolling up his sleeves. His friend asks, "Why the hell did you throw my dollar in the toilet?"
The Pollack said, "I dropped a quarter in there, and I'm not sticking my hand in all that shit just for a quarter!"

*   *   *

A Polish guy orders a pizza and they ask him he would like that cut into eight slices or sixteen. He says, "Better make it eight. I'm not that hungry."

*   *   *

Why is there a fence around Poland?

To keep the dogs from peeing on the Poles.

*   *   *

A polish guy gets a job as an inspector with the Mars company. He's assigned to the M&M division. When hardly any candies where making it to the end of the assembly line, they found out why. It was because he was throwing away all the Ws.

*　　　　*　　　　*

How'd the Polack break his arm raking leaves?

He fell out of the tree.

*　　　　*　　　　*

How many Polacks does it take paint a house?

One thousand and one. One to hold the brush and a thousand to lift the house up and down.

*　　　　*　　　　*

How many Polacks does it take to change a light bulb?

Five. One to hold the bulb and four to turn the ladder.

*　　　　*　　　　*

How many Polacks does it take to make popcorn?

Six. One to hold the pan and five to shake the stove.

*　　　　*　　　　*

A Polish guy rents a chain saw from Home Depot and returns it three days late. The tool rental guy informs him that he could have bought one for these rental charges. "Why did it take you so long?" The Polack said, "I think this thing needs sharpening. It took me all this time to cut down one tree." The rental guy starts it up to make sure it's in working order and the Polack shouts, "What's that noise?"

MEXICANS

(Manuel Labor Blows!)

* * *

An Irishman, an Italian and a Mexican all work as iron workers on top of a tall skyscraper. They eat lunch together every day. One day the Irishman opens his lunch box and yells, "Corned beef again? If I have to eat this shit one more day I'm gonna kill myself!" The Italian opens his lunch box. "Spaghetti again? One more day of this and it's good night for Tony!" The Mexican open his lunch and yells, "Tamales again? I'm sick of this ca-ca! One more day of this and I'm going to kill myself too!"

The next day the Irishman opens his lunch box. "God damn that woman! I hate boiled meat!" He jumps to his death. The Italian opens his and starts cursing at his spaghetti. He too jumps to his death. The Mexican opens his and finds more tamales. "Chinga!" He jumps.

At the joint funeral all the widows were huddled together crying. The Irish wife shouts to the heavens, "If I had only listened to his complaints he'd still be with us!"

The Italian wife says,""Why didn't I listen? I could have made him a sandwich!" The Mexican's wife yells, "Don't look at me. He packs his own lunch!"

* * *

What do you get when you cross an African American and a Mexican?

Someone that's too lazy to steal.

*   *   *

Why don't Mexicans cross the border in threes?

The sign says NO TRESPASSING.

*   *   *

What do Mexican women and hockey goalies have in common?

They both change their pads after three periods.

*   *   *

What's the difference between a park bench and a Mexican?

A park bench can support a family of four.

*   *   *

What did Davy Crockett say when he saw all those Mexicans coming towards the Alamo?

"Who ordered concrete?"

*   *   *

What do you call a Mexican baptism?

Bean dip.

*   *   *

How are Mexicans like a cue ball?

The harder you hit them, the better english you get.

*   *   *

Why do Mexicans suck at the game Uno?

They keep stealing the green cards.

*   *   *

Did you hear about the new Mexican game show?

'So you think you can mow?'

*   *   *

A guy puts an ad in the paper looking for a painter. A Mexican knocks on his door. "Senior, you looking for painter? I painter." The man told him he was in the middle of an important, long distance phone call. "Just go around back and start on the porch. There is a couple of gallons of green paint, brushes and rollers. I'll be with you in a few minutes."

A few minutes later the Mexican knocks on his door again and says, "Senior, I feeny." "You feeny? Oh, you're finished?" "Si. I finished." "That was quick. You painted the whole porch already?" "Si. But you no have no porch. You have Mercedes!"

PUERTO RICAN
(Spic n spans)

*   *   *

Radio contest Grand prize: A week in Puerto Rico.

Second place prize: Two weeks in Puerto Rico.

*   *   *

What do you get if you cross a Puerto Rican and a Chinaman?

A car thief that can't drive.

*   *   *

How do you get a Puerto Rican pregnant?

Cum on her shoes and let the flies do the rest.

*   *   *

A young, very pregnant Puerto Rican girl is told by her mother that the sex of the child depends on the sexual position during conception. "If the man is on top it will be boy. If the woman is on top, it will be a girl." The girl bursts into tears. "Oh snap! I'm having puppies!"

*   *   *

Why don't Puerto Ricans play hide and seek?

Who would look for them?

*   *   *

The priest asks at the matrimony, "Do you Maria, take Salvador Francisco Antonio Ricardo Alvarez do be your lawfully wedded husband?" Maria speaks up quickly, "NO! You must have the wrong wedding. I'm just marrying Sal!"

*   *   *

What do you call a Puerto Rican midget?

A speck.

*   *   *

What's so great about being a Puerto Rican Jew?

If you can't talk them down in price, you just steal it.

*   *   *

Why do Puerto Ricans make great laxatives?

They irritate the shit out of everyone.

*   *   *

What do you call a Puerto Rican with no hands?

Trustworthy.

*   *   *

What did the Puerto Rican name his second son?

Hose B.

*   *   *

Why wasn't Jesus born in Puerto Rico?

Nobody could find three wise men or a virgin.

*   *   *

Why aren't there any Puerto Rican doctors?

It's hard to write a prescription with spray paint.

*   *   *

What's the difference between a dead Puerto Rican and a dead dog in the road?

There are skid marks in front of the dog.

BLACKS
(Back of the bus; Back of the book)

*   *   *

What do you call a white guy with two black guys?

Referee.

*   *   *

What do you call a white guy with three black guys?

Victim.

*   *   *

What do you call a white guy with five black guys?

Coach.

*   *   *

What do you call a white guy with ten black guys?

Quarterback.

*   *   *

What do you call a white guy with a thousand black guys?

Warden.

*   *   *

What word begins with the letter N, ends with the letter R and you never, EVER want to call a black person this?

Neighbor.

*   *   *

Little Leroy was helping his momma bake a cake. He smeared some flour on his face. "Momma, Momma! Look, I'm a white boy!" Momma smacks him and kicks him out of the kitchen. He goes into the den. "Papa look! I'm a white boy!" His dad whips his ass and sends him to his room. He passes Granny's room. "What's that stuff on your face boy?" "I'm a white boy Granny!" Grandma spanks his ass. Leroy cries, "I've only been white for two minutes and I already hate all you spooks!"

*   *   *

What do you call an epileptic African American prostitute with braces?

A Black and Decker Pecker Wrecker.

*   *   *

A black guy, a Mexican and a white guy found a lamp and a genie came out and granted each one wish. The black guy said he would like all the black people to move back to Africa and live in peace and harmony. 'Poof!' His wish was granted. The Mexican guy wishes that all his people would return south of the border to escape all the racism in this country. 'Poof!' He too gets his wish. The genie asked the white guy what he would like. The white guy says, "How bout a beer?"

*   *   *

Why do so many black people live in Detroit?

There's no jobs there.

*   *   *

Two black guys driving cross country get pulled over by a Texas State Trooper. The cop, with a big ol' cowboy hat, walks up to the drivers side and motions for the driver to roll down his window. Before the driver reaches the handle, the cop smashes the window with his baton. "I said roll down the window! Now, get out of the car!" Before the guy can even pull the door handle the cop grabs him by the neck and jerks him out through the broken glass. He stands him on his feet and says, "I said get out of the car boy! You better start following instructions! Now, let me see some I.D.!" Before the driver can get his wallet out of his pocket the cop shoves him over the roof of the car, picks him up and slams him against the trunk. "Show me some I.D. NOW BOY!" The guy takes out his license and hands it to the officer as fast as he could. The cop takes his I.D. to run through his dashboard computer.

He returns a few minutes later and hands him his license back and tells him he's free to go. The cop walks around to the passenger side and makes a motion for the other guy to roll down his window. He rolls down the window right away. The cop leans in and punches the passenger in the face, breaking his nose. Reeling in pain, "Hey man! What did you do that for?" The cop answers, "I'm just granting your wish." "My wish? What the hell are you talking about?" The cop explains, "Once you got a mile down the road you were going to say to your buddy, "I wish that white mother-fucker tried that shit on me!"

*   *   *

At a fancy penthouse party a few guys were discussing the power of the winds whipping between the buildings. "You know these thermals drawing the wind straight up can support the weight of a grown man," one says. The black guy calls, "Bullshit!" "No, really. Watch." The guy stands up on the ledge, feels the winds rushing up on his outstretched hand and jumps. He falls about twenty stories and floats right back up to the ledge. He says to the black guy, "Now you try it. It's fun!" The black guy steps onto the ledge, reaches out to feel the wind and jumps. He plummets to his death. The third guy says, "Damn Superman, you fuckin hate them, don't you?"

*   *   *

A woman asked the only black guy in the bar if it was true what they say about black guys. He says, “Yeah.”
She said, “Prove it!”
So he stabbed her and took her purse.

*   *   *

Tyler (a white guy) and Tyrone (a black guy) move into their new houses right next to each other. The next summer Tyler put up a picket fence and Tyrone copied him. The following summer Tyler put in a pool. So did Tyrone. Tyler painted his house. Tyrone painted his the same color. Tyler got pissed off and put up a For Sale sign. Tyrone put up a For Sale sign asking twice as much. Tyler asked Tyrone, "Why do you think your house is worth twice as much as mine?" Tyrone said, "My neighbor’s not black.”

*   *   *

If a black guy and a Mexican are in a car, who's driving?

The cops.

*   *   *

An eighteen wheeler delivering bowling balls to the new lanes stalls on top of a hill, the rear doors open under pressure from the weight shift and all the bowling balls dump out and start rolling down the hill. The truck driver, at a loss for what to do, starts chasing after them. At the bottom of the hill a group of Klu klux klan members start smashing them with sledge hammers. "STOP! What are you doing to my bowling balls?" They all said in unison, "Bowling balls, bullshit! We're going to kill these Africans before they hatch."

*   *   *

What are four things a black guy can't get?

A taxi, a black eye, a fat lip, a job.

*   *   *

Two girls from Louisiana go into a novelty, old time photo shop. They dress up like women from the old west. The photographer is using one of those old fashioned cameras that you have to put your head under the hood. The girls are holding their pose wondering what's taking so long. "I think he's trying to focus," one says. The other asks, "Both us?"

*　　　*　　　*

What's long and hard on a black guy?

Second grade.

*　　　*　　　*

Why do black guys always have sex on their minds?

Because they have pubic hair on their head.

*　　　*　　　*

Two black guys are down and out. Sitting on the curb pissing and moaning about how bad it sucks to be black. "Man, if we was white, it would be so great. I'd have a big house, a nice car and a job." One of them notices a sign on a storefront offering a color change. 'Today's special: White. Only nine dollars!'
"Man, we should do that! How much cash you got?" "I got a ten." "Shit! I only got eight." They sat there depressed. One of them says, "Man, I know what we should do! Ask a white guy!" They ask the next white guy that walked by. The white guy says, "You take your ten, go in first and then give him your change then he'll have nine. Good luck." "Man, that guy is smart. Let's do this!"
The first guy goes in and comes out an hour later a caucasian. Nice suit, new shoes and an attache case. His friend is amazed how great he looks. "Hey man. You got that dollar?" His friend replied, "Get a job nigger!"

* * *

How many black guys does it take to shingle a roof?

One. But you gotta slice him real thin.

* * *

What's the difference between Batman and a black man?

Batman can go out at night without Robin.

* * *

What does Pontiac stand for?

Poor Old Nigger Thinks It's A Cadilac.

* * *

What do you call a black guy that stutters?

Cocoon.

* * *

How do you know Adam and Eve were white?

Have you ever tried taking a rib from a black guy?

* * *

Why is Stevie Wonder always smiling?

He doesn't know he's black.

*   *   *

What does a Christmas tree and a black guy have in common?

They both have colored balls.

*   *   *

What do you call a black woman that has an abortion?

A crime stopper.

*   *   *

Why weren't there any black people in The Flintstones?

They haven't evolved yet.

*   *   *

Why weren't there any black people in The Jetsons?

We got rid of them by then.

*   *   *

If a black guy and a Puerto Rican both jumps off the same building at the same time, who hits the ground first?

Who cares?

* * *

What's FI, FY, FO, FO, FI, FY, FO?

Mike Tyson's phone number.

* * *

What does Mike Tyson do after sex?

Washes the pepper spray from his eyes.

* * *

How was break dancing invented?

Black kids stealing hubcaps off of moving cars.

* * *

If a black guy and a Iranian both jump off the same building at the same time, who hits the ground first?

The black guy. The Iranian is a shade lighter.

* * *

Why was six afraid of seven?

Because seven was black.

*   *   *

Why don't black kids play in the sandbox?

Because the cats always bury them.

*   *   *

What do you say to an African American wearing a suit?

Would the defendant please rise?

*   *   *

Why do black folks keep chickens around the yard?

To teach their kids how to walk.

*   *   *

A girl says to a black guy in the club, “Is that a coke can in your pocket or are you just glad to see me?”

He says, “No. It’s my chapstick.”

*   *   *

What do you do with a dead black guy?

Skin him and use for a wet suit.

*　　　*　　　*

How can you tell if a black person has been using your computer?

It’s gone.

*　　　*　　　*

Did you hear about the black owned French restaurant in New Orleans?

It's called, Che' Whaaat?

*　　　*　　　*

What do you get when you cross a black guy and a billy goat?

A weedeater that won't work.

*　　　*　　　*

What did the black kid get for Christmas?

Your bike.

*　　　*　　　*

How many black people does it take to change a light bulb?

Now how are you going to count them in the dark?

*   *   *

Why do black people hate aspirin?

They're white. They work. You have to pick cotton to get to them.

*   *   *

What's the difference between black people and snow tires?

Snow tires don't sing when you put chains on them.

*   *   *

Why are all the black people you know so fast?

The slow ones are in jail.

*   *   *

What do you call the brown spots on the bottom of elephants' feet?

Slow natives.

*   *   *

How is life like a box of jelly beans?

Nobody likes the black ones.

* * *

Why don't black people like chain-saws?

When you start them, they go..."Rrrrrun! nigger nigger. Rruunn!"

* * *

How do you stop a black kid from running around?

Wet his lips and stick him to the wall.

* * *

How do you stop a black kid from jumping on the bed?

Put velcro on the ceiling.

* * *

How do you get him down from the ceiling?

Tell him the Mexicans are coming to use him for a piniata.

* * *

What did the black kid get on his S.A.T. exam?

Barbecue sauce.

*   *   *

A black guy walks into a bar with a parrot on his shoulder. The bartender says, “Hey cool! Where did you get him?” The parrot says, “In Africa. There’s millions of them.”

*   *   *

What would Martin Luther King be doing if he was white?

Living.

*   *   *

Three third graders, a Jew, an Italian and a African American were on the playground and they decided to play a game, ‘Who has the biggest dick?’ They laughed at the Jewish kid. The Italian’s was at least two inches longer. The African American whipped his out and really impressed the other kids. It was WAY bigger than the theirs.

That night during supper the African American’s mom asked what he did in school today. “We played ‘Who’s got the biggest dick.’ I won. The other kids say it’s because I’m black. Do you think that’s true momma?” She said, “No. It’s because you’re twenty two.”

*   *   *

A black guy goes into a bar and orders a drink. A gay guy walks up and offers him a blow job. The black guy punches him in the face, grabs him by the neck and drags him outside and beats his ass. He comes back in, sweaty and out of breath. He takes his seat again. The bartender asks him, "What was that about?" The black guy says, "I don't know. He said some shit about giving me a job!"

*   *   *

How did the mayor of New York improve the transportation problem in Harlem?

He moved the trees closer together.

*   *   *

What do you call a black guy that flies a plane?

A pilot. You racist.

*   *   *

Bubba is browsing in a Louisiana pawn shop and finds a gold rat on the shelf. He turns it over to check the price and it's so heavy that he almost dropped it. He asked the pawnbroker if it was real gold. The shop owner assures him it is. “It's only two hundred dollars but there is a story that goes with it. The story is a thousand dollars.” The guy says, "Nah, I'll just take the rat." As he's walking home with this heavy bag he looks back and sees a real rat following him. He starts walking faster and after he turned the corner he looked back again and now there's a dozen rats following him. He picks up speed but the rats are increasing in numbers and gaining on him. The guy takes off running full sprint but so are the rats. By the hundreds now. He runs down to the bayou and throws the gold rat in the water. All the rats follow it into the water and drown. The guy walks back to the pawn shop drenched in sweat. The pawnbroker, with a grin on his face, asks, "I bet you want that story now, don't you?"
He says, "Fuck the story! You got any golden Africans?"

*   *   *

George Burns turned one hundred years old and is doing the rounds on all the talk shows. While on Oprah, she began the interview, "Mr. Burns, you are one hundred years old yet you still drink, smoke cigars and carouse with women. How do you do it?" George Burns told her, "Come back to my dressing room after the show and I'll show you how I do it." That got a huge laugh from the audience.

After the show, Oprah knocked on his dressing room door. "Mr. Burns, I'm here for you to show me how you do it." The door swung open, he grabbed Oprah and threw her down on the bed. He yanked her dress up over her head and started fucking the shit out of her. She's flailing around in disbelief. "Hold my balls bitch!" he shouts. She reaches down and grabs hold. He's plowing the hell out of her. He has to tell her again, "Hold my balls, don't let go!" She tries to follow orders but again she loses grip from the pounding and can only hold onto the bed for dear life. "Squeeze by balls bitch! Don't let go!" She grabs hold with all her might and he busts a tremendous nut and she has the best orgasm she's ever had in her life.

He gets up and starts getting dressed but she can hardly get her vision back to normal. She's lying there out of breath with her hair all fucked up. "Mr. Burns, that was the most amazing sex I've ever had! But why did you want me to hold your balls?"

He said, "The last sister I boned stole my wallet."

*   *   *

And we all lived happily ever after anyway.

Now go away!

20840441R00128

Made in the USA
Middletown, DE
11 December 2018